A
SCOTTISH
MISCELLANY

This edition published 2009 by Waverley Books,
David Dale House, New Lanark, ML11 9DJ

Text by Michael Bruce

ISBN 978-1-902407-78-4

Printed and bound in the UK

Acknowledgements
This book would not have been completed without the
many contributions and fastidious research of Judy Hamilton

Thanks must also go to Scott Simpson for his contributions,
and to Shona Moir, Danny Maloney, Neil Wylie,
Ronnie Hamilton, Keith Hawley, Nell Brownlee and Richard Bowen

Folding of the great kilt, illustrations by Mark Mechan

'Flower of Scotland' copyright © The Corries (Music) Ltd
and reproduced with permission

'Scotland the Brave' copyright © The Estate of Cliff Hanley and reproduced
with the permission of the Hanley family

Illustrations of The Broons and Oor Wullie
copyright © DC Thomson & Co Ltd, and reproduced with permission

The translation of the Declaration of Arbroath, 1320, is found in the National
Archives of Scotland, Edinburgh and is © Crown copyright

Information on Glasgow street gangs courtesy of James McGowan

Thanks to Richard McPherson of Strathclyde Passenger Transport,
www.spt.co.uk, and to Carolyne Nurse of St Andrews Links Trust

John Hughes' Glasgow Cup Winner's medal 1964–65,
courtesy of David Convery, Convery Auctions Ltd.

Willie Lyon's Scottish Football Association Winner's medal 1936–37,
courtesy of Stephen McDermott

scottishmiscellany@geddesandgrosset.co.uk

A SCOTTISH MISCELLANY

MICHAEL BRUCE

WAVERLEY BOOKS

SCOTTISH MONARCHS

From the unification of Scotland to the Union of the Crowns (1603)

1005–1034	Malcolm II	1249–1286	Alexander III
1034–1040	Duncan I	1286–1290	Margaret
1040–1057	Macbeth	1292–1296	John Balliol
1057–1058	Lulach	1306–1329	Robert I Bruce
1058–1093	Malcolm III	1329–1371	David II
1093–1094	Donald Ban	1371–1390	Robert II
1094	Duncan II	1390–1406	Robert III
1094–1097	Donald Ban (restored)	1406–1437	James I
1097–1107	Edgar	1437–1460	James II
1107–1124	Alexander I	1460–1488	James III
1124–1153	David I	1488–1513	James IV
1153–1165	Malcolm IV	1513–1542	James V
1165–1214	William	1542–1567	Mary
1214–1249	Alexander II	1567–1603	James VI

- Longest reigning king of Scotland: William – 49 years (James VI's rule was longer, lasting from 1567–1625 (58 years) but from 1603, he ruled as king of Scotland *and* England.)
- Shortest reigning king of Scotland: Duncan II (7 months)
- Youngest Scottish monarch: Mary Queen of Scots. She became Queen when she was seven days old.

SCOTTISH MONARCHS – ALSO KNOWN AS

Malcolm III	'Canmore' (from Gaelic 'ceann mor' – 'big head')
Alexander I	'The Fierce'
David I	'The Saint'
Malcolm IV	'The Maiden' (he did not marry)
William I	'The Lion'
Margaret	'The Maid of Norway'
John Balliol	'Toom Tabard' (Empty Coat)
James V	'The King o' the Commons'
James VI	'The Wisest Fool in Christendom'
James VII	'The King o'er the Water'

THE FAMILY TREE
OF THE SCOTTISH MONARCHY

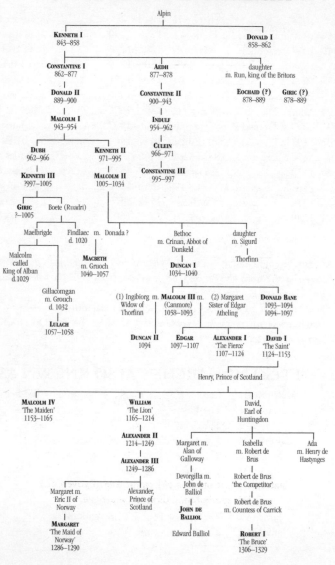

Alpin

KENNETH I
843–858

DONALD I
858–862

CONSTANTINE I
862–877

AEDH
877–878

daughter
m. Run, king of the Britons

DONALD II
889–900

CONSTANTINE II
900–943

EOCHAID (?)
878–889

GIRIC (?)
878–889

MALCOLM I
943–954

INDULF
954–962

DUBH
962–966

KENNETH II
971–995

CULEIN
966–971

KENNETH III
?997–1005

MALCOLM II
1005–1034

CONSTANTINE III
995–997

GIRIC
?–1005

Boete (Ruadri)

Maelbrigde

Findlaec m. Donada ?
d. 1020

Bethoc
m. Crinan, Abbot of
Dunkeld

daughter
m. Sigurd

Malcolm
called
King of Alban
d.1029

MACBETH
m. Gruoch
1040–1057

DUNCAN I
1034–1040

Thorfinn

Gillacomgan
m. Grouch
d. 1032

(1) Ingibiorg m. **MALCOLM III** m. (2) Margaret
Widow of   (Canmore)   Sister of Edgar
Thorfinn   1058–1093   Atheling

DONALD BANE
1093–1094
1094–1097

LULACH
1057–1058

DUNCAN II
1094

EDGAR
1097–1107

ALEXANDER I
'The Fierce'
1107–1124

DAVID I
'The Saint'
1124–1153

Henry, Prince of Scotland

MALCOLM IV
'The Maiden'
1153–1165

WILLIAM
'The Lion'
1165–1214

David,
Earl of
Huntingdon

ALEXANDER II
1214–1249

Margaret m.
Alan of
Galloway

Isabella
m. Robert de
Brus

Ada
m. Henry de
Hastynges

ALEXANDER III
1249–1286

Devorgilla m.
John de
Balliol

Robert de Brus
'the Competitor'

Margaret m.
Eric II of
Norway

Alexander,
Prince of
Scotland

**JOHN DE
BALLIOL**

Robert de Brus
m. Countess of Carrick

MARGARET
'The Maid of
Norway'
1286–1290

Edward Balliol

ROBERT I
'The Bruce'
1306–1329

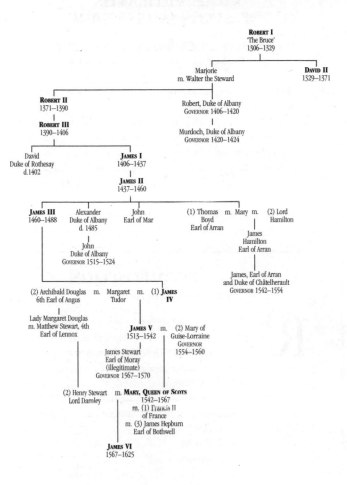

Dates are those of reign of king or rule of governor.
The symbol m. indicates a marriage.

VIOLENT DEATHS
OF KINGS JAMES I TO V

James I   Murdered in the royal lodgings at Blackfriars Perth, in 1437 by Sir Robert Graham as a result of a conspiracy led by the Earl of Atholl.

James II   Killed by an exploding cannon while supervising the seige of Roxburgh castle in 1640.

James III   Murdered in 1488 after the Battle of Sauchieburn in which the king was opposed by a force led by his 15-year-old son, James IV. It had been prophesied that he would be betrayed by his nearest kin and James III had imprisoned his brother as a result.

James IV   Killed at the battle of Flodden Field in 1513 as he advanced into England in support of the French and the 'auld alliance'.

James V   Died of grief after his defeat at the battle of Solway Moss in 1542.

ROYAL DECOMPOSITION
Did you know ...?

Robert III had a riding accident when he was young, which left him disabled. His physical weakness was matched by a lack of strength of character. He was considered unfit to rule in his own right and his brother, the Duke of Albany, effectively ruled in his place.

Robert had a very low opinion of himself – so low, it seems, that it was his wish to be buried in a dung heap! His chosen epitaph should have read:

'Here lies the worst of kings and
the most miserable of men'.

As usual, however, nobody paid any attention to him and he was laid to rest in Paisley Abbey.

MAJOR ART GALLERIES AND MUSEUMS

The Aberdeen Art Gallery
The Burrell Collection, Glasgow
The Centre for Contemporary Arts (CCA), Glasgow
The City Art Centre, Edinburgh
The Dean Gallery, Edinburgh
Dundee Art Galleries and Museum
The Gallery of Modern Art, Glasgow
The Glasgow School of Art
The Hunterian Museum and Art Gallery, Glasgow
The Inverness Museum and Art Gallery
Kelvingrove Art Gallery and Museum, Glasgow
The Kirkcaldy Museum and Art Gallery
The Lighthouse, Glasgow
The McLellan Gallery, Glasgow
The McManus Galleries, Dundee
The Museum of Childhood, Edinburgh
The Museum of Flight, East Fortune, East Lothian
The Museum of Scotland, Edinburgh
The Museum of Scottish Country Life, Wester Kittochside near East
    Kilbride
The Museum of Transport, Glasgow
The National Gallery of Scotland, Edinburgh
The National War Museum of Scotland, Edinburgh Castle
The Paisley Museum and Art Galleries
The People's Palace, Glasgow
The People's Story, Edinburgh
Pollok House, Glasgow
Provand's Lordship, Glasgow
The Queen's Gallery, Holyrood House, Edinburgh
The Royal Museum, Edinburgh
The Royal Scottish Academy, Edinburgh
Saint Mungo's Museum of Religious Life and Art, Glasgow
The Scottish National Gallery of Modern Art, Edinburgh
The Scottish National Portrait Gallery, Edinburgh
The Stirling Smith Art Gallery and Museum, Stirling
The University of Dundee Museum Collections
The Writer's Museum, Lady Stair's House, Edinburgh

MUSEUMS OF EMPLOYMENT AND INDUSTRY

The Aberdeen Farming Museum
The Aberdeen Maritime Museum
The Buckie Drifter Maritime Heritage Centre, Buckie
Dalgarven Mill Museum, Kilwinning, Ayrshire
Fordyce Joiner's Workshop, Aberdeenshire
Leadhills Miners' Library, Leadhills
The Museum of Lead Mining, Wanlockhead
New Lanark Mills, World Heritage Site
Paisley Museum and Art Gallery (Paisley shawls collection)
Preston Mill, East Lothian
Sandhaven Mill Visitor Centre, Aberdeenshire
The Savings Bank Museum, Ruthwell, Dumfries and Galloway
The Scottish Fisheries Museum, Anstruther
The Scottish Maritime Museum, Irvine, Ayrshire
The Scottish Mining Museum, Newtongrange, Midlothian
Strachur Smiddy, Argyll
The Verdant Works, Dundee
The Weaver's Cottage Museum, Airdrie, Lanarkshire

MUSEUMS DEDICATED TO FAMOUS SCOTS

(JM) Barrie's Birthplace, Kirriemuir, Angus
The John Buchan Centre, Broughton, near Biggar, Lanarkshire
The Robert Burns Centre, Dumfries
Burns' Cottage, Alloway
Burns' House Museum, Mauchline
Thomas Carlyle's Birthplace, Ecclefechan
Andrew Carnegie's Birthplace Museum, Dunfermline
The Jim Clark Room, Duns, Borders
John Paul Jones Birthplace Museum, Kirkbean, Dumfries and Galloway
The William Lamb Memorial Studio, Montrose
The David Livingstone Collection, Blantyre
Mary Queen of Scots' House, Jedburgh
Hugh Miller's Cottage, Cromarty
The James Paterson Museum, Moniaive, Thornhill, Dumfries and Galloway
Sir Walter Scott's Courtroom, Selkirk, Scottish Borders
The [John] McDougall Stuart Museum, Dysart, Fife

THE GLASGOW FOUR

Charles Rennie Mackintosh (1868–1928)
James Herbert MacNair (1868–1955)
Frances Macdonald (1874–1921)
Margaret Macdonald (1865–1933)

In the late nineteenth century, a group of four students at the Glasgow School of Art met and began to work together. Their collaborative work, which was strongly influenced by the Arts and Crafts Movement, Japanese art, symbolism and Art Nouveau in Europe, emerged as a new and exciting style – 'The Glasgow Style'. It was initially received more enthusiastically on the continent than in Great Britain, but in time 'The Four' emerged as leaders of the Art Nouveau movement in Scotland. They applied their skills to a variety of design projects including metalwork, furniture, illustration and interiors. The group separated when Herbert MacNair and Frances Macdonald, who married in 1899, moved to Liverpool. Charles Rennie Mackintosh and Margaret Macdonald married in 1900 and continued to work together on a number of influential projects, including the Willow Tearooms in Glasgow. Of the four, it was Charles Rennie Mackintosh who emerged as the greatest star – architect, interior designer and artist. He designed buildings with meticulous attention to detail, giving as much consideration to items of furnishing and details of interior decoration as to the external design. The Glasgow School of Art and the Hill House in Helensburgh are two outstanding examples of Mackintosh's work.

THE SCOTTISH COLOURISTS

Francis Campbell Boileau Cadell (1833–1937)
John Duncan Fergusson (1874–1961)
George Leslie Hunter (1877–1931)
Samuel John Peploe (1871–1935)

A name given to a group of four Scottish artists working in the early decades of the twentieth century. All of them had spent time studying in France and were strongly influenced by Post-Impressionism, particularly the work of Matisse, the Fauves and Cezanne. The Colourists' originality and progressive approach, and their profound influence on Scottish painting, have only been fully recognised in retrospect. Their work is characterised by a strong emphasis on colour and light in their paintings, and fluid handling of paint.

THE GLASGOW SCHOOL

Joseph Crawhall (1861–1913)
Thomas Millie Dow (1848–1919)
Sir James Guthrie (1859–1893)
George Henry (1858–1943)
Edward Atkinson Hornel (1864–1933)
William Kennedy (1859–1918)
Sir John Lavery (1856–1941)
William York Macgregor (1855–1923)
Arthur Melville (1855–1904)
James Stuart Park (1862–1933)
James Paterson (1854–1932)
Alexander Roche (1861–1921)
Edward Arthur Walton (1860–1922)

In the late nineteenth century, a group of artists began to form in Scotland, whose work was characterised by a new realism, naturalism and a bolder style of painting. The artists were strongly influenced by the work of the French painters of the period, in particular Jules Bastien-Lepage. They gathered in groups to paint together outdoors (in Scotland and in France) and in the studio, sharing resources and ideas. Several of them exhibited their work together. The 'father' of the group is generally recognised as WY Macgregor and the other leading figures were Lavery and Guthrie. The work of the Glasgow School, as it came to be known, spanned a period of less than twenty years but was profoundly influential on Scottish art. The above artists are associated with the Glasgow School.

POPULATION OF SCOTLAND
(CENSUS RESULTS) 1801–2001

1801 – 1,608,000
1811 – 1,805,864
1821 – 2,091,521
1831 – 2,364,386
1841 – 2,620,184
1851 – 2,888,742
1861 – 3,062,294
1871 – 3,360,018

1881 – 3,735,573
1891 – 4,025,647
1901 – 4,472,103
1911 – 4,670,904
1921 – 4,882,497
1931 – 4,842,980
1941 – NO CENSUS
1951 – 5,096,415

1961 – 5,179,344   1991 – 5,102,400
1971 – 5,228,963   2001 – 5,062,011
1981 – 5,130,735

TARTAN DAY

It's a strange thing, but St Andrew's Day is celebrated more by Scots abroad than in their own country. The Scots abroad are more patriotic than those at home. In the United States of America and Canada in particular, thousands of people of Scots descent take a great deal of pride in the significant part that the Scots emigrants have played in their country's history. In addition to St Andrew's Day and Burns Day, another date has entered the calendars of those of Scots ancestry in the USA and Canada. In recognition of the Scots' contribution to the shaping of both countries, Tartan Day is now officially recognised as a day of celebration. It was first celebrated nationally in Canada in 1993 and in 1997, the United States followed suit. It was officially recognised by a Resolution of the American Senate in 1998. The chosen date for celebrating Tartan Day is April 6th. It was on this day in 1320 that the Declaration of Arbroath was signed. The American Declaration of Independence was modelled to a considerable extent on the Declaration of Arbroath. Tartan Day is now a day when all organisations in Canada and the US with Scottish connections pay tribute to famous and influential Scots in their country's past, to the contributions they made in politics and government, education, science and many other spheres of human activity.

CASTLES

- Last castle to be besieged in Great Britain: Blair Castle, Perthshire (1746).
- Most northerly castle in Scotland: Muness Castle, Unst, Shetland.
- Most northerly mainland castle: Castle Girnigoe and Sinclair, north of Wick. A seat of the Sinclair Earls of Caithness.
- Castle most likely to appear on calendars: Eilean Donan Castle, Argyll.
- Most westerly castle: Kisimul Castle, Castlebay, Barra, stronghold of the MacNeils.
- Largest inhabited castle: Floors Castle, near Kelso, home of the Duke of Roxburgh.
- Oldest inhabited castle in Scotland: Traquair House, by Innerleithen, Peeblesshire.

- Most haunted castle in Scotland (allegedly): Glamis Castle, Tayside. Ghosts include 'Earl Beardie', who was said to have played cards with the Devil, a monstrous 'family secret' who was rumoured to be kept in a hidden room, and Janet Douglas, who was burned for witchcraft in the sixteenth century.
- Only triangular castle in Great Britain: Caerlaverock Castle, near Dumfries.
- Royal palaces: Dunfermline Palace, Edinburgh Castle, Falkland Palace, Linlithgow Palace, The Palace of Holyroodhouse, Stirling Castle.
- Current Royal Residences in Scotland: Balmoral Castle, The Palace of Holryroodhouse.

SCOTTISH CASTLES AS FILM LOCATIONS

Blackness Castle, West Lothian	*Hamlet* (1990), *Ivanhoe* (BBC TV 1997), *Macbeth* (1997), *The Bruce* (1996) *Bonnie Prince Charlie* (1948)
Ardverikie Castle, Kinlochlaggan, near Aviemore, Highland	*Monarch of the Glen* (BBC TV 1999–2005)
Castle Kennedy, Stanraer, Dumfries and Galloway	*The Wicker Man* (1973)
Culzean Castle, Ayrshire	
Doune Castle, Doune, Stirling	*Ivanhoe* (BBC TV 1997), *Monty Python and the Holy Grail* (1975)
Duart Castle, Isle of Mull	*Entrapment* (1999)
Dumbarton Castle, West Dunbartonshire	*Gregory's Two Girls* (1999)
Dunnottar Castle, near Stonehaven, Aberdeenshire	*Hamlet* (1990)
Duns Castle, Berwickshire, Scottish Borders	*Mrs Brown* (1997)
Eilean Donan Castle, Dornie, Highland	*The World is Not Enough* (1999) *Highlander* (1986), *Highlander 3* (1994) *Highlander: Endgame* (2000), *Loch Ness* (1996), *Entrapment* (1999)
Floors Castle, Kelso, Scottish Borders	*Greystoke* (1984)
Lauriston Castle, Edinburgh	*The Prime of Miss Jean Brodie* (1969)

Manderston Castle, Duns, Borders	*The House of Mirth* (2000)
Morton Castle, Dumfries and Galloway	*The Thirty-Nine Steps* (1978)
Neidpath Castle, Dumfries and Galloway	*The Bruce* (1996)
Castle Stalker	*Monty Python and the Holy Grail* (1975)
Stirling Castle, Stirling	*Kidnapped* (1971), *Gregory's Two Girls* (1999), *Tunes of Glory* (1960)

SCOTTISH GLENS AS FILM LOCATIONS

Glen Coe	*Braveheart* (1995), *Rob Roy* (1995), *Monty Python and the Holy Grail* (1975), *Harry Potter and the Prisoner of Azkaban* (2004), *Bonnie Prince Charlie* (1948), *Kidnapped* (1960)
Glenfinnan	*Bonnie Prince Charlie* (1948), (viaduct) *Harry Potter and the Chamber of Secrets* (2002), *Charlotte Gray* (2001)
Glen Nevis	*Kidnapped* (1960), *Harry Potter and the Philosopher's Stone* (2001), *Braveheart* (1995), *Highlander 3* (1994)
The Sma' Glen	*Chariots of Fire* (1981)

OTHER FILM LOCATIONS

Young Adam (2003)	Forth and Clyde Canal
The House of Mirth (2000)	Glasgow: City Chambers, Theatre Royal
Trainspotting (1996)	Edinburgh
Local Hero (1983)	Arisaig, Morar, Moidart, Pennan
Whisky Galore (1949)	Island of Barra
Gregory's Girl (1980)	Cumbernauld
Highlander (1986)	Loch Sheil, Torridon, Skye
The Wicker Man (1973)	Burrow Head, Plockton, Kirkcudbright
Breaking the Waves (1996)	Skye, Mallaig
The Thirty-nine Steps (1978)	Balquidder, Killin, Dunblane, Forth Rail Bridge

Chariots of Fire (1981)   Edinburgh, St Andrews
Mrs Brown (1997)   River Pattack, Lochan na h-Earba
Monty Python and the Holy Grail (1975) Rannoch Moor, Loch Tay
Festival (2005)   Edinburgh city centre
Enigma (2001)   Oban, Loch Feochan

RELIGIOUS BUILDINGS

- The Declaration of Arbroath was signed in Arbroath Abbey, in 1320.
- The first Cistercian community in Scotland was at Melrose Abbey.
- The largest cathedral ever built in Scotland was St Andrews Cathedral, St Andrews, Fife. Building commenced in 1160 and the cathedral was consecrated in 1318.
- The smallest cathedral in Scotland is the Cathedral of the Isles (Scottish Episcopal), in Millport on the Isle of Cumbrae. The cathedral seats 70 people.
- The oldest Christian Settlement in Scotland is Whithorn Priory.
- The oldest complete cathedral in Scotland is Glasgow Cathedral.
- The oldest Roman Catholic diocese in Scotland is the Diocese of Galloway.
- The oldest Post-Reformation church still in use in Scotland is Burntisland Parish Church. It was at a General Assembly at Burntisland in 1601 that James VI's proposal for an English translation of the Bible (which was to become the Authorised Version) was approved.
- The only medieval monastery in Scotland which is still inhabited is Pluscarden Abbey, Elgin (Benedictine, founded 1230).
- The only Post-Reformation Cistercian community in Scotland is at Nunraw Abbey, Haddington, East Lothian (established 1946).
- Testament to the Clearances – victims of the clearances who took refuge in Croik Church in Sutherland, scratched their names into the glass of the church windows. The names can still be seen today.
- St Magnus Cathedral in Orkney is the most northerly cathedral in Scotland.
- The first Buddhist monastery built in Scotland is Samye Ling, Eskdale Muir. It was founded in 1967.
- There is now a Buddhist retreat on Holy Island. The island was purchased in 1992. In 2003, the island's Peace Centre opened.
- The Central Mosque in Glasgow was purpose-built and opened in 1984.
- The Central Mosque in Edinburgh was completed in 1998.
- There are mosques in Aberdeen, Dunfermline and Dundee.

MEDIEVAL ABBEYS OF SCOTLAND

Abbey	founded	faith
Arbroath Abbey	1178	Tironesian
Ardchattan Priory	1230	Valliscaulian
Balmerino Abbey	1229	Cistercian
Beauly Priory	1230	Valliscaulian
Cambuskenneth Abbey	12th century	Augustinian
Crossraguel Abbey	1244	Cluniac
Culross Abbey	1217	Cistercian
Deer Abbey	1219	Cistercian
Dryburgh Abbey	1152	Premonstratensian
Dundrennan Abbey	1142	Cistercian
Dunfermline Abbey	*c.*1070	Benedictine
Fearn Abbey	*c.*1227	Premonstratensian
Glenluce Abbey	1190	Cistercian
Holyrood Abbey	*c.*1128	Augustinian
Holywood Abbey	*c.*1180	Premonstratensian
Inchcolm Priory	1123	Augustinian
Inchmahome Priory	1238	Augustinian
Iona Abbey	1200	Benedictine
Jedburgh Abbey	1138	Augustinian
Kelso Abbey	1128	Tironesian
Kilwinning Abbey	12th century	Benedictine
Kinloss Abbey	1151	Cistercian
Lindores Abbey	12th century	Benedictine
Melrose Abbey	1130	Cistercian
Newbattle Abbey	1140	Cistercian
Paisley Abbey	1163	Cluniac
Pluscarden Abbey	1230	Valliscaulian
Restenneth Priory	1153	Augustinian
Saddell Abbey	1160	Cistercian
Selkirk Abbey	1113	Tironesian
Sweetheart Abbey	1273	Cistercian

SCOTTISH COMIC CLASSICS:
THE DANDY AND THE BEANO

Publisher: DC Thomson, Dundee
First issue of *The Dandy*: November 1937
First issue of *The Beano*: July 1938

MEMORABLE CHARACTERS AND ORIGINAL
ILLUSTRATORS: THE BEANO

character	introduced	illustrator
Lord Snooty	July 1938	Dudley D Watkins
Big Eggo the Ostrich	July 1938	Reg Carter
Biffo the Bear	January 1948	Dudley D Watkins
Dennis the Menace	March 1951	David Law
Rodger the Dodger	April 1953	Ken Reid
Little Plum	October 1953	Leo Baxendale
Minnie the Minx	December 1953	Leo Baxendale
The Bash Street Kids (originally called 'When the Bell Rings' till 1956)	1954	Leo Baxendale
Jonah	March 1958	Ken Reid
Billy Whizz	May 1964	Malcolm Judge
Gnasher (Dennis's dog)	1968	David Law
Baby Face Finlayson	April 1972	Ron Spencer
Rasher (Dennis's pet pig)	1979	David Sutherland
Ivy the Terrible	May 1985	Robert Nixon
The Germs	January 1988	David Sutherland

MEMORABLE CHARACTERS AND ORIGINAL
ILLUSTRATORS: THE DANDY

character	introduced	illustrator
Korky the Cat	1937	James Crichton
Desperate Dan	1937	Dudley D. Watkins
Hungry Horace	1937	Allan Morley
Keyhole Kate	1937	Allan Morley
Winker Watson	1961	Terry Bave
Black Bob	1944	(text story)
Danny Long Legs	1944	Dudley D. Watkins
Plum McDuff	1948	Bill Holroyd

Rusty	1950	Paddy Brennan
General Jumbo	1953	Paddy Brennan
Screwy Driver	1955	Bill Holroyd
Robin Hood	1958	Paddy Brennan
Spunky and his Spider	1968	Bill Holroyd
Corporal Clott	1960	David Law
Big Head and Thick Head	1963	Ken Reid
Jack Silver	1973	Bill Holroyd
Cuddles and Dimples	1986	Barry Appleby

SCOTTISH COMIC CLASSICS: THE BROONS

Creator	Dudley D Watkins (1907–1969)
Publisher	DC Thomson, in *The Sunday Post*
Date of Birth	8th March 1936. Two generations of the Broon family were born on the same day: Maw and Paw Broon and their children, Joe, Hen, Maggie, Daphne, Horace, the Twins and the Broon Bairn. The oldest member of the Broon family, Granpaw, was born some months later, in September.

Paw Broon Has worn the same suit since 1936. Balding, with a walrus moustache. An affectionate and well-meaning father and husband, but not very bright.

Maw Broon Rarely seen without her pinny on, unless she is going out, when she wears a coat and sometimes a hat. Has worn her hair in a bun since 1936. Long-suffering manager of the family.

Hen Broon The tall, dark, lanky one. Usually wears a striped suit. Joined the army during World War II.

Joe Broon Shorter and stockier then Hen Broon. Fair-haired. Wears a plain suit. Like Hen, he served his country during the war.

Maggie Broon The glamorous one. Never seen without her lipstick. Compared to most of the others in her family, she has a large and varied wardrobe.

Daphne Broon Dark-haired, plump and less glamorous than her sister Maggie. Always does her best to dress well, as she is ever hopeful of finding a 'click'.

Horace Broon The earnest, bespectacled brains of the family. Always wears school uniform.

The Broon Twins   Identical, sometimes troublesome. What are their names? One was referred to as Eck in a 1940 strip. Sometimes they are referred to as 'ae Twin' and 'the ither Twin'.

The Broon Bairn   In spite of the fact that she is the youngest and never changes her dress, the Bairn often manages to appear as the most mature, sensible and level-headed member of the family.

Granpaw Broon   Easily identified by his characteristic white beard and walrus moustache, his dark suit and his bunnet. An old rascal who can be more trouble than all the children put together.

Address   10, Glebe Street.
Holiday home   The But an' Ben.

OOR WULLIE: A POTTED MISCELLANY

Creator   Dudley D Watkins (1907–1969)
Publisher   DC Thomson, in *The Sunday Post*
Date of Birth   8th March 1936
Family   Ma, Pa and Oor Wullie. In early strips, Wullie had a wee brother but he disappeared without explanation.

Friends PC Murdoch (sometimes).
Wullie also knows the Broons.
Primrose is his girlfriend.

His gang Wee Eck, Soapy Soutar, Fat Bob.

Enemies PC Murdoch (sometimes).
Pet Jeemy (Moose). Harry the terrier
is a modern addition.

Favourite dress Dungarees and tackety boots.
Favourite food Ma's mince and tatties and clootie
dumpling – braw!

Favourite sayings 'Jings!' 'Crivvens!' 'Help ma
boab!'
Favourite seat His bucket.

- Contrary to urban folklore, according to Broons scriptwriter David Donaldson, no mention of Wullie's second name has been made in any of the strips.
- After Dudley D Watkins' death, Ken H Harrison (b. 1940) drew both the Broons and Oor Wullie. Peter Davidson is the current artist.

GLASGOW STREET GANGS

While the city of Glasgow may have been the 'Second City of Empire' – a place of commerce, heavy industry and manufacturing, and an international *entrepot* – it has also been, for the past 200 years, a place with something of a reputation for street violence.

Glasgow is not, of course, the only place in Scotland to have possessed unruly citizenry – the Edinburgh mob was much feared in its day – but it seems that the combination of a large working class population with great poverty and vast areas of substandard housing has produced a lasting tradition of gangs and fighting, the only real difference over the years being in the declining age of the gang members.

Glasgow gangs were first recorded in the 18th century, when there was a weekly ritual fight between rival gangs on the banks of the Clyde opposite the city centre. These gangs became known later as the 'penny mobs', due to their co-operative habit of charging members a subscription fee of a penny a week, to set against any fine imposed by the courts on an arrested member.

By the start of the 20th century, the courts had taken to jailing violent wrong-doers, and so the penny mob lost its purpose, but the gangs endured, and post-World War I, large-scale gangs like the Billy Boys, the Norman Conks and the Redskins came to the fore. Their violent rivalry was characterised by the use of cut-throat razors and widespread sectarianism – the infamous Glasgow razor gangs were born. Generally, you could tell the religious affiliation of a gang, if not from its name, then certainly by its territory, and woe betide you if you got it wrong.

In the 1950s and '60s, as the poorer population was relocated en masse into the new sprawl of public housing, gang membership and activity fell away, only to start increasing again in the following decades. This time, however, the members were not so much the young adult men of the district, but bored, distracted and rebellious teenagers, and this time also, gang activities would stray away from organised crime and violence. To be sure, gangs would still be agressively territorial, and would happily fight each other, but now, just as often, acts of violence and vandalism would be entirely random, often visited upon the innocent, and spurred on by alcoholism and drug abuse.

Since the 1980s, gang motifs like the tweed cap of the Redskins have been replaced by a uniform of skip cap, shell suit and trainers, together with heavily gelled short hair and consumption of bottles of an archetypal tonic wine.

Gang names, on the other hand, very often reflect their ancient forebears. Those including 'tong' or 'toi' are tracing a connection to the original San Toi of the east end. Indeed, so many adopted the name that the original gang changed theirs to 'Real Calton Tongs', a gang that exists to this day. Junior versions often used the prefix 'young', 'young young', 'tiny' and even 'toddler', while female versions use 'she', 'lady' or, an '80s emergence, 'posse'.

A SELECTION OF GLASGOW GANGS

Gang	Location
Antique Mob	Shettleston
Apostles	Ferguslie Park
Auchinairn Young Team	Auchinairn
Aunty	Possil
Baby Cumbie	Castlemilk, Gorbals
Baby Tongs	Calton
Baltic Fleet	Bridgeton
Bar-G	Bargeddie
Bar-L	Barlanark
Bears	Govanhill
Bellway Fleeto	Drumchapel
Big Bar-L	Barlanark
Big Do'ehill	Calton
Billy Boys	Bridgeton, Haghill
Bison	Auchinairn, Balornock, Bishopbriggs, Kirkintilloch
Black Hand Gang	Calton
Black Muffler	Clydebank
Blackhill Coby	Blackhill
Bloodhound Flying Corps	Hutchestontown
Bobby's Boys	Partick
Boot Boys	Govanhill
Border Bandits	Dennistoun
Borheed Mad Squad	Barrhead
Borrheed Bowery	Barrhead
Bowery	Barrhead
Bowrie	Whiteinch
Bridgegate Boys	Gallowgate
Brigton Derry	Bridgeton

Gang	Location
Bundy	Castlemilk, Clydebank, Kirkintilloch, Pollok, Drumry, Pollokshaws
Butney Boys	Maryhill
Calton Entry Boys	Calton
Car-D	Cardonald
Carntyne Crew	Carntyne
Catholic Young Team	Garngad, Parkhead, Provanmill
Chinatoon	Hallglen
Choir Boys	Scotstoun
Coburg Erin	Gorbals
Cody	Maryhill, Cranhill
Cowboys	Denniston
Cow Toi	Cowcaddens
Craig	Castlemilk
Crew	Pollok
Cross Young Team	Partick
Cumbies	Gorbals
Cyto	Cadder, Cranhill, Garngad, Gorbals, Partick, Provanmill
Dale Street Boys	Bridgeton
Dead Dogs	Partick
Den Toi	Easterhouse
Derry Boys	Bridgeton
Dirty Dozen	Gorbals
Drag	Easterhouse, Lochend
Drummy	Drumchapel, Easterhouse, Lochend
Drygate Youths	Drygate

Gang	Location	Gang	Location
Duke Street Firm	Dennistoun	Mini Team	Govan
Duntoker Fleeto	Duntocher	Mini Tongs	Calton
Eminent	Calton	Moors	Paisley, Renfrew
Fleet	Castlemilk, Cranhill,	Mummies	Maryhill
	Finnieston, Knightswood,	Nitsie	Nitshill
	Maryhill, Partick, Possil,	Norman Conks	Bridgeton
	Scotstoun, Anniesland,	Nunny	Bridgeton
	Garscadden, Greenfield,	9 Krew	Pollok
	Queenslie, Ruchazie	Paisley Mad Squad	Paisley
Gestapo	Denniston	Parlour Boys	Gorbals
Glen	Rutherglen	Peel Glen Boys	Drumchapel
Gold Dust Gang	Gorbals	Pigs	Possil
Goucho	Carntyne	Pirates	Cranhill
Govanhill Young Team	Govanhill	Plum Boys	Bridgeton
Gringo	Barmulloch	Pollok Young Team	Pollok
Hammer Boys	Gorbals	Port Toi	Port Dundas
Hell's Troops	Paisley	Potty Mob	Priesthill
Hill	Govanhill	Powery	Haghill
Himshie	Cambuslang	Priesty	Priesthill
Home Boys	Larchgrove	Psychie Young Young	Baillieston
Hutchie	Hutchestontown,	Queens Cross Boys	Maryhill
	Croftfoot, Oatlands, Polmadie	Real Calton Tongs	Calton
K Gang	Bridgeton	Rebels	Pollok, Possil, Queenslie,
Kent Star	Calton		Rutherglen, Tradeston
Kirky	Kirkintilloch	Redskins	Anderston, Bridgeton,
Krew	Pollok		Calton, Finnieston,
Lady Buck	Drumchapel		Gallowgate, Gorbals,
Lady Bundy	Pollok		Mile End, Townhead, Tradeston
Lady Govan Team	Govan	Remo	Renfrew
Lady Toi	Cowcaddens,	Roman Catholic Tongs	Calton
	various areas	Rutherglen Wild Team	Rutherglen
Local Defence Volunteers	Haghill	San Toi	Calton
Lochy-Crewe	Lochend	Saracen Tongs	Hamiltonhill
Maryhill Boot Squad	Maryhill	Seedhill Young Team	Paisley
Maryhill Young Team	Maryhill	Shamrock	Garngad,
Mealy Boys	Gorbals		Germiston, Roystonhill
Midget Moors	Paisley, Renfrew	Shanghai Boys	Bridgeton
Mini Bar-L	Barlanark	She Bar-L	Barlanark

Gang	Location	Gang	Location
She Fleet	Maryhill	Valley	Castlemilk, Maryhill
She Toi	Calton, Castlemilk, Easterhouse	Vambo	Bridgeton
		Village Boys	Baillieston, Gorbals
She Tongs	Calton	Vordo	Govan
Shields	Pollokshields	Vyto	Baillieston, Maryhill
Shotgun Remo	Renfrew	Wee Cumbies	Gorbals
Silver Bell	Unknown	Wee Men	Parkhead, Tollcross
Skid Row	Barlanark	West End Posse	Maryhill
Skull	Burnside, Cathcart, Toryglen	West Rebels	Easterhouse
Spacemen	Govan	WIFTY	Fernhill
Star	Kinning Park	Wild Young Catholic Shamrock	Garngad
Stickit Boys	Bridgeton	Wimpey	Dalmuir
Suicide Hun	Paisley	Wine Alley	Govan
Tay	Castlemilk	Y41	Easterhouse, Lochend
The Fleet	Bridgeton	Young Cow Toi	Cowcaddens
Tigers	Shettleston	Young Cumbie	Gorbals
Tim Malloys	Calton	Young Fleet	Anniesland
Tiny Cumbie	Gorbals	Young Partick Fleeto	Partick
Tiny Glen	Rutherglen	Young Posso Fleeto	Possil Park
Tiny Monks	Dennistoun	Young Powery	Haghill
Tiny Tongs	Calton	Young Remo	Moorpark
Tiny Young Powcry	Haghill	Young Riddrie Team	Riddrie
Toddler Tongs	Calton	Young Ruchill Boys No.1	Ruchill
Toi	Bishopbriggs, Blackhill, Calton, Castlemilk, Cowcaddens, Haghill, Port Dundas, Toryglen, Whiteinch, Yoker	Young Ruchill Joy Riders	Ruchill
		Young Ru'glen Scheme Team	Rutherglen
		Young Sighthill Team	Sighthill
Toi Soldiers	Calton	Young Southie	South Nitshill
Tongs	Calton	Young Springburn Peg	Springburn
Toon	Pollokshaws, Arden, Carnwadric, Mearns Village, Shawlands	Young Team	Castlemilk, Gorbals, Govan, Govanhill, Knightswood, Maryhill, Pollok
Toryglen Young Team	Toryglen	Young Tongs	Calton
Tradeston Young Rebels	Tradeston	Young Toon	Arden, Carnwadric, Townhead
Tummel Toi	Riddrie		
21 Krew	Pollok	Ziggy Fleet	Ruchazie
Uncle	Possil		

SCOTTISH FARE

ATHOLL BROSE

According to legend, this drink was first concocted in the fifteenth century by the Duke of Atholl. The Duke was hot in pursuit of Iain Macdonald, the rebellious Lord of the Isles. He had found where the rascal was hiding out with his men, and wanted to stall him to await reinforcements. The Duke discovered the site of the well from which Macdonald and his men were drinking and ordered it to be filled with a mixture of whisky, oatmeal and honey. Not surprisingly, having drunk of the magical 'waters', the bold Macdonald was lulled into a sense of warm security and was quite happy to stay where he was until the Duke of Atholl had him captured.

There are various versions of the recipe for Atholl Brose. According to some recipes, the oatmeal should be stirred into the brose, but it is more commonly soaked and strained and the resultant liquor alone is used, as below. The measurements of the ingredients can be adjusted according to individual taste.

Ingredients

100g oatmeal
2 cups water
2–3 tablespoons runny Scottish heather honey
whisky

Stir the oatmeal into the water in a bowl. Leave to stand for at least half an hour to allow the oatmeal to absorb the water and swell. Stir again. The mixture should resemble a thick paste. Pour into a muslin cloth and squeeze over another bowl, until all liquor has been removed. Discard the oatmeal. Stir the honey into the oatmeal liquor and add enough whisky to make up to approximately two litres. Bottle. Shake well before pouring.

Aberdeen Angus: A Scottish breed of beef cattle, that have an international reputation for the quality and flavour of their meat.

Arbroath Smokies: Whole haddock, salted and smoked over wood chips, named for their place of origin. Usually sold as a brace, tied at the tail. Simply heat through in the oven and serve with warm, buttered oatcakes.

DEEP-FRIED MARS™ BAR

It's difficult to accept, whatever the popular folklore, that any Scottish chip shop owner actually made this. It is, possibly, a concoction aimed at conspiring to highlight the Scots' unconditional love for fried food (for it does not love us back) and our renowned culinary services to heart disease. That said, deep-fried pizzas – and deep-fried, battered pizzas (Pizza Crunch) – do genuinely appear in some Lanarkshire chip shops, so the existence of the deep-fried Mars™ bar, though in all likelihood an urban myth, is unfortunately not completely beyond belief. More frightening than anything is that this recipe works and that it is sickly sweet but delicious. 'Fun-size' bars might be a more sensible idea than the large ones. Serve as dessert with vanilla ice-cream, or see the option below.

    1 Mars™ bar, chilled overnight in the
       refrigerator
    self-raising flour
    fizzy mineral or soda water
    oil for deep frying

Sieve the flour into a bowl and slowly add, whisking with a fork, as much cool, fizzy mineral water as will make a thick, creamy batter. Heat the oil in a deep-fat fryer. Drop a little batter into the oil to test the temperature. If the batter bubbles and quickly turns brown then it is ready. Completely cover the bar in batter, drop into the hot oil and cook till golden brown (about three minutes).

Serve with chips for a fully balanced, nutritional meal.

Atholl Brose: A whisky-based drink with oatmeal and honey.

Bannocks: Most often, another name for oatcakes (q.v.), but also appearing as a type of soda scone, and as Selkirk bannock (q.v.). The word 'bannock' apparently comes from the anciently called area of that name, around Stirling.

Black Bun: A rich cake made with flour, dried fruits, treacle, milk and spices, encased in pastry. Traditionally eaten at New Year.

Bridies: Meat and onions encased in a folded circle of flaky pastry. The town of Forfar is famed for its bridies.

Butteries: Morning rolls made with a yeast dough, lard and butter. Greasy, salty, but delicious (and long lasting), they are popular in the north-east of Scotland. Traditionally associated with Aberdeen.

Clapshot: A simple dish from Orkney – mashed potato and turnip (swede), with butter, herbs and seasonings.

Clootie Dumpling: A pudding made from flour, dried fruit, treacle, milk and spices, tied in a cloth and boiled. Often eaten with the main course, and as a fried slice.

Cock-a-Leekie: A traditional Scottish soup. The principal ingredients are chicken stock, potatoes and leeks.

Crail Capon: A haddock

Cranachan: A dessert made with whisky, oatmeal and cream. Raspberries may also be added.

Crappet Heads: Tastier than it sounds, this haddock soup includes fishballs, which are for some reason stuffed into cleaned out fish heads before being boiled.

Crowdie: Delicate whey cheese, rolled in oatmeal.

Cullen Skink: A chowder made with smoked haddock and potatoes.

Deep-fried Mars™ bar: A (possibly urban mythical) chip shop delicacy where an already calorie-laden chocolate bar is dipped in batter and deep-fried. Sounds appalling, but, worryingly, is surprisingly nice.

Dundee Cake: A rich, fruity cake topped with almonds, popular in the nineteenth century.

Edinburgh Fog: A typically Scottish dessert, comprising vast quantities of double cream and sugar, flavoured with almonds and whisky liquer.

Finnan Haddies: Smoked haddock fillets of a golden hue (*never* yellow), best dotted with butter and lightly baked in a dish of milk. They give their name to a Scottish country dance tune, and even turn up in the lyrics of Cole Porter, who was obviously getting rather desperate for more rhymes for 'My Heart Belongs to Daddy'. When the Titanic sank, she took 100lbs of Finnan haddies with her in the kitchen stores.

Glasgow Salad: Apocryphally, this is said to consist of pie, beans and chips, the pie almost certainly being a Scotch pie (q.v.).

Gourock Ham: Salted herring.

Haggis: A pudding of oatmeal and mutton offal, generally considered to be the national dish of Scotland, and a lot nicer than one might think.

Herrings in Oatmeal: Herrings coated in rough oatmeal and fried.

Hotchpotch: A thick broth made with mutton and vegetables.

Hot Toddy: Whisky-based 'cure all'.

Howtowdie: Roast chicken, cooked with a stuffing of skirlie (q.v.). It is traditionally served with poached eggs.

Jeely Piece: A jam sandwich, as in the famous song of that name (*'Oh, ye cannae fling pieces oot a twenty-storey flat...'* etc.)

Jethart Snails: Boiled sweets, originating from the Borders town of Jedburgh. They are twists of dark-brown boiled toffee.

Kale Soup: Kale, type of cabbage, was a mainstay vegetable for many Scots, particularly in the Highlands. This traditional recipe includes barley and beef with the kale.

Kedgeree: It is maintained that a Scottish regiment serving in India was the point of origin for this Victorian breakfast dish of rice, smoked haddock, eggs and curry spices.

Kippers: Whole herring, split and smoked. Strongly flavoured archetypal Scottish fare, but not for everyone. Scottish waters used to support thousands of herring drifters – small fishing boats. These days, herring are something of a delicacy.

Lorne Sausage: Pork or beef sausagemeat shaped in a loaf tin and sliced prior to frying or grilling.

Marzipan Dates: Stoned dates, stuffed with marzipan and rolled in sugar – definitely one for Christmas.

Mealie Pudding: A sausage-shaped pudding made from oatmeal, onions and dripping which is served as an accompaniment to meat.

Millionaire's shortbread: Shortbread covered in caramel and chocolate and cut into bars. A tray-bake favourite all over Scotland.

Mince and Tatties: Another candidate for *the* Scottish fare – sautéed beef mince with onions, served with mashed potato. A filling and warming dish for the winter months. In some neighbourhoods yet, you can smell the mince cooking at the end of the day.

Moffat Toffee: a very dark, hard toffee with a distinctive, treacly, almost burnt taste. Available from the famous Moffat Toffee Shop, in the borders town of that name.

Oatcakes: Oat biscuits, which are sometimes flavoured with cheese, traditionally made on a griddle.

Partan Bree: A soup made with crabmeat, chicken or fish stock, rice and cream. Partans are small, edible crabs, and a bree is basically a stock, so it is a well-titled dish.

Porridge: An important staple in the Scottish diet for hundreds of years.

Porridge was originally made with coarse oatmeal, which was boiled in water until it formed the consistency of a rough, thick custard. Nowadays, most porridge is made from porridge oats, which do not take so long to cook. It is traditionally flavoured with salt, but can also be eaten with sugar or honey and milk, or cream.

Potted Hough: Beef shin bone, simmered for several hours in water with seasoning. The meat is removed from the bone and shredded after cooking, then potted with the reduced stock (strained), which sets to a jelly when it cools.

HAGGIS

The following is a haggis recipe taken from *Mistress Margaret Dods' Cook and Housewife' Manual*, first published 1826, revised and enlarged 1829. Meg or Margaret Dods was the pseudonym of Christian Isobel Johnstone (1781–1857) a writer and editor, a name she took from the fictional landlady of the Cleikum Inn in Sir Walter Scott's novel *St Ronan's Well*. This inn was the venue of the meetings of the Cleikum Club, a dining club where members gathered to celebrate Scottish literature, culture and customs. As a work of fiction the book is introduced by a long story involving several other characters from St Ronan's and contains numerous footnotes concerning the club. The book was first dismissed as a literary joke, but the revised edition of 1829 came to be held as a useful household manual and a source for many delicious authentically Scottish recipes.

Most countries have a spicy aromatic sausage dish such as haggis but it's fame as Scotland's national dish has more to do with its association with Robert Burns than with any prestige on its part. Despite the trepidation many people feel for the eating of haggis – which is understandable when reading the rather medieval preparation below – there are many quite delicious modern recipes on the market and even an award-winning vegetarian version.

'Clean a sheep's pluck [stomach] thoroughly. Make incision in the heart and liver to allow the blood to flow out, parboil the whole [heart, liver and lungs], letting the windpipe lie over the side of the pot top, permit the phlegm and blood to

---

disgorge from the lungs: the water may be changed after a few minutes for fresh water. A half-hour's boiling will be sufficient: but throw back half of the liver and boil till it will grate easily. Take the heart, half of the liver and part of the lights [lungs, heart and liver], trimming away all the skins and black looking parts, and mince them together. Mince also a pound of good beef suet and four or more onions. Grate the other half of the liver. Have a dozen small onions peeled and scalded in water to mix with the mince. Have ready some finely-ground oatmeal, toasted slowly before the fire four hours, till it is of a light brown colour and perfectly dry. Less than two teacupfuls of meal will do this quantity of meat. Spread the mince on a board and stew the meal lightly over it, with a high seasoning of pepper, salt, and a little cayenne, first well mixed. Have a haggis bag, perfectly clean, and see that there is no thin part in it, else your labour will be lost by its bursting. Some cooks use two bags, one as an outer case. Put the meat with half-pint of good beef-gravy, or as much strong broth as will make it very thick stew. Be careful not to fill the bag too full, but allow the meat room to swell; add the juice of a lemon, or a little good vinegar; press out the air and sew up the bag; prick it with a large needle when it first swells in the pot to prevent bursting; boil it slowly for three hours if large. This is a genuine Scotch Haggis; the lemon and cayenne may be omitted, and instead of beef gravy, a little of the broth in which the pluck is parboiled may be taken.

'A finer Haggis may be made by parboiling and skinning sheep's tongues and kidneys, and substituting these minced for most of the lights, and soaked bread or crisped crumbs for toasted meal. There are moreover sundry modern refinements on the above recipe – such as eggs, milk, pounded biscuits, etc. – but these by good judges are not deemed improvements. Some cooks use the small tripes in making lamb's haggis.'

PORRIDGE

Porridge is one of the healthiest ways to start the day. Oats is an energy-giving superfood, and despite Dr Johnson's derision that it was 'a grain which in England is generally given to horses but in Scotland supports the people', porridge will fill you up from early morning right through till the afternoon.

To be authentically Scottish, porridge should be made with coarse or pinhead oatmeal rather than rolled oats. If you want to be totally authentic, the milk should not be poured over the porridge but poured into a separate bowl and each spoonful of porridge cooled in the bowl of milk. This makes sure the milk stays as cold as possible.

Traditionally, leftover porridge, confusingly referred to in the plural as 'they' (the oats), would in working households have been poured into a kitchen drawer, left to cool and cut into slices for the men to take to work. It might also have been fried and served with eggs for dinner.

And of course 'they' should only be seasoned with salt. In truth, I think it's safe to claim that perfectly traditional additions to porridge would be honey or treacle. But the addition of salt to oats really brings out its flavour, so be sure to include a good pinch of salt no matter what sweet topping you prefer.

Ingredients

1 cup of coarse or pinhead oatmeal
3 cups of cold water
Salt

Soak the oatmeal overnight (if you are using rolled oats then there is no need to do this). The following day, add a good pinch of salt and bring the oatmeal slowly to the boil. Stir the oatmeal continuously with a wooden spoon or a spurtle (a wooden stick for this purpose) and serve when thick and creamy. Serve with full fat milk and a further sprinkling of salt (or the sweet topping of your choice).

RUMBLEDETHUMPS

The relative quantities of the ingredients can vary according to personal preference. Quantities of cheese depend very much on how strong your cheese is and how much cheese you like. This is reportedly Prime Minister Gordon Brown's favourite dish.

Ingredients

Potatoes, boiled and mashed (approx 750g)
Cabbage (approx 500g), cut into strips or
 small pieces
One large onion, diced
Scottish cheddar cheese (approx 100g)
Butter (approx 30g)
Black pepper

1 Gently fry the cabbage and onion in butter until soft.
2 Mix cabbage and onion into the mashed potato and stir in half of the cheese, and plenty of black pepper.
3 Place the mixture in an ovenproof dish and sprinkle the remaining cheese on top. Bake in a hot oven until piping hot and the cheese is golden and bubbling.

A teaspoonful of hot mustard, stirred into the potato before it is mixed with the other vegetables, makes a tasty, if unorthodox, addition to this warming supper dish.

Rumbledethumps: A supper dish made from potatoes, onions and cabbage.

Scones: Small, unyeasted buns with a distinctive, dry taste. Delicious with sweet or savoury fillings. Varieties include cheese, fruit and treacle.

Scotch Broth: A thick soup made with mutton stock, barley, onions, carrots, turnip and dried peas.

Scotch Egg: An old picnic favourite – a boiled egg wrapped in sausagemeat and rolled in breadcrumbs.

Scotch Pie: The native hamburger – minced lamb or mutton in a suet pastry, baked in a hand-sized mould. As the pie lid is recessed, there is room to add some embellishments. Mashed potato, baked beans and brown sauce are among the favourites. There are some filling variations, too - steak, curry and macaroni cheese. Truly a food of the people.

WHISKY HOT TODDY

This may not be a cure, but it certainly is one of the most effective means of comforting a cold. The honey and the lemon juice are soothing to the throat and the whisky is soothing to the spirits! Don't waste good malt whisky – use a blended brand.

Ingredients

50ml Scotch whisky (approx)
50ml boiling water (approx)
The juice of half a lemon
One teaspoonful of heather honey

Stir the honey and lemon juice together in a heatproof glass. Add the boiling water and stir until the honey is dissolved. Add the whisky and stir again.

Selkirk Bannock: A fruit bread, rather than a bannock, first made by a Selkirk baker to use up leftover dough and traditionally reserved for Christmas.

Sheep's Heid: A sheep's head, so it is said, makes a nourishing meal for several people, particularly if cooked in a broth with vegetables and barley, although it is rather daunting in appearance.

Shortbread: A rich, buttery biscuit, traditionally cooked in rounds and cut into triangles (petticoat tails).

Skirlie: a stuffing made of seasoned pinhead oatmeal and fried onions.

Soda Scones: Griddle scones made with flour, milk and bicarbonate of soda.

Soor Plooms: Boiled sweets, green in colour and sour in flavour.

Steak Pie: A new year tradition holds that one must be able to provide oneself, and any visitors, with a hearty meal and this is usually steak pie, made of stewed steak, gravy, onions and puff or shortcrust pastry.

Stovies: A thick stew, traditionally made with potatoes and onions, cooked slowly on the stove top with lard or beef dripping. Sausages, corned beef, leftover roast meat, or mince may also be added. It is always plural.

Tablet: Butter and sugar, to which is added condensed milk. The resultant boiling, once cooled in a tray, should be hard as nails, yet melt in the mouth. An ability to make good tablet has been the social making of many a genteel lady.

Tattie Scones: Patties of mashed potato and flour, usually shaped into triangles and griddled. Best warmed through, but some people fry them.

PRITCHARD THE POISONER

Forty years ago in England Dr Pritchard he was born,
Little his parents thought he'd die in Glasgow town in scorn;
Satan surely tempted him, as I must plainly say,
His loving wife and mother-in-law now lie mouldering in the clay.

Anon., Saturday morning, July 29, 1865

The lines above are from a song written after Glasgow's last public execution. It took place at the Saltmarket, July 28, 1865, and around 100,000 attended. Dr Edward William Pritchard (1825–1865) had been found guilty of the poisoning of his wife and mother-in-law.

In 1864, Pritchard made his family's 15-year-old servant girl pregnant. He carried out an abortion on the girl, and promised her that he would marry her should his wife die. In November of that year his wife Mary became ill with symptoms of vomiting and dizziness. Her mother came to look after her and also came down with the same symptoms. Mary died in February and her mother died a month later. Their death certificates were both prepared by Pritchard. Following an anonymous letter to the Procurator Fiscal the bodies were exhumed and an autopsy showed death by poisoning. Pritchard was arrested and the evidence against him was overwhelming.

THE AMERICAN DECLARATION OF INDEPENDENCE: SCOTLAND'S PART

It is thought that as many as twenty-one, maybe more, of the men who signed the American Declaration of Independence had Scottish blood. Two of the signatories – John Witherspoon (the only clergyman to sign) and James Wilson – were born in Scotland. Among the signatories who had Scots forebears were Thomas Jefferson, Thomas McKean, Francis Lewis, Phillip Livingston, George Ross and Benjamin Rush.

BASIC SCOTTISH COUNTRY DANCE STEPS

1 Pas de Basque (a setting step for reels and jigs).
2 Schottische (a setting step for Strathspeys).
3 Skip change of step (a travelling step) – either beginning with a hop, (reels and jigs) or ending with a hop (Strathspey).
4 Slip step (for circling with partner or whole set in reels or jigs).
5 Step up/step down (for changing position within the set).

LOCHS

- Largest loch (surface area): Loch Lomond.
- Largest loch (volume of water): Loch Ness.
- Deepest loch: Loch Morar (1077ft/328m deep).
- Longest inland loch: Loch Awe, Argyll (25 miles/41km long)
- Longest sea loch: Loch Fyne, Argyll
- Loch famed for seafood: Loch Fyne, Argyll.
- Lochs linked by the Caledonian Canal: Loch Dochfour, Loch Ness, Loch Oich, Loch Lochy.
- Vanished loch: The Nor' Loch, Edinburgh. The Nor' Loch, now the site of Princes Street Gardens, was originally created in the fifteenth century as part of the town's defences. It soon became a stinking pool where the worst of the city's refuse was deposited. It was clearly a health hazard and was drained in the eighteenth century when Edinburgh's New Town was built.
- Scotland's only lake: The Lake of Menteith, Perthshire.

LOCH MONSTERS

Everyone has heard of Nessie, the monster who is said to inhabit the waters of Loch Ness. Many people are also aware of the alleged existence of Morag, the monster of Loch Morar. Nessie and Morag are not the only ones, it would seem. There are quite a number of lochs around Scotland where monsters have allegedly been sighted. Some of the monsters have been given names.

Loch Arkaig, Knoydart (Archie)
Loch Assynt, Ross-shire
Loch Awe, Argyll
Loch Beiste, Wester Ross
Cauldshields Loch, Borders
Loch Duvat, Eriskay
Loch Fyne, Argyll
Loch Eil, Inverness-shire
Loch Laggan, Inverness-shire
Loch Linnhe, Inverness-shire
Loch Lochy, Great Glen (Lizzie)
Loch Lomond, Stirlingshire
Loch Meikle, near Drumnadrochit
Loch na Mna, Rasay

Loch Oich, Great Glen (Wee Oichy)
Loch Quoich, Inverness-shire (Quoichy)
Loch Rannoch, Perthshire
Loch Shiel, Lochaber (Shielagh)
Loch Tay, Perthshire
Loch Trieg, Trossachs
Loch Vennachair, Rasay

GERMAN SHIPS SCUTTLED AT SCAPA FLOW

Following the 1918 armistice of the First World War it was agreed that the warships of the German Navy would be interned at Scapa Flow in the Orkney Islands. Over seventy German ships were disarmed, manned with a minimum crew and sailed to what had been Britain's main naval base. Admiral Ludwig von Reuter, deprived of news from Germany and with final treaties not yet signed, suspected that the armistice negotiations would break down and that he and his crews would be captured. On June 21, 1919 he gave the order that every ship at Scapa Flow should be scuttled (deliberately sunk) to prevent them from being captured by the British. Most of the wrecks have been salvaged over the years for their valuable metals, although a few still remain and are popular diving sites.

Dreadnoughts
Baden
Bayern
Friederich der Grosse (flagship)
Grosser Kurfürst
Kaiser
Kaiserin
König
König Albert
Kronprinz Wilhelm
Markgraf
Prinzregent Luitpold

Battlecruisers
Derfflinger
Hindenburg
Moltke

Scydlitz
Von der Tann (S)

Light Cruisers
Nürnberg
Frankfurt
Karlsruhe
Köln
Dresden
Bremse
Emden (flagship)
Brummer (S)

Destroyers
1st Flotilla
G38 (S)
G39 (S)

G40 (Leader)

G86 (S)

S32 (S)

V129 (S)

2nd Flotilla

B110 (leader)

G101

G103

V100

B109

B111

B112

G104

3rd Flotilla

S54 (leader)

S55

G91

V70

V73

V81

V82

6th Flotilla

S131

S132

S49

S50

V125

V126

V127

V128

V43

V44 (leader)

V45

V46

7th Flotilla

G89

G92

H145

S136

S137

S138 (leader)

S36

S51

S52

S56

S60

S65

V78

V80

V83

ROADS

- Highest road in Scotland: Bealach Na Ba (Pass of the Cattle), from Tornapress to Applecross.
- Longest major road in Scotland: A9 (Edinburgh – Scrabster)
- First motorway in Scotland: The M8. Construction began in 1964.
- Motorways
  M8 (Edinburgh–Glasgow),
  M9 (Edinburgh–Bridge of Allan),
  M73 (M74 Glasgow–A80 Moodiesburn)
  M74 (Glasgow–Gretna)
  M77 (M8 Glasgow–A77 East Renfrewshire)

M80 (M8 Glasgow–A80 Garnkirk)
M876 (M9–A80 Longcroft)
M898 (M8 Glasgow–A898 Erskine Bridge)
M90 (Inverkeithing–Perth)

DANGEROUS ROADS

According to a survey carried out in 2002 by the European Road Assessment Program, supported by the AA (Britain) Foundation for Safety Research, the A889 near Dalwhinnie is the most dangerous stretch of road in the UK. According to calculations based on motor vehicle accident statistics, the seven most dangerous roads in Scotland are listed in the following order:

1 A889 near Dalwhinnie (A86–A9)
2 A99 (A9 Latheron–Wick)
3 A82 (Tyndrum–Tarbert)
4 A86 (Spean Bridge–A9 Kingussie)
5 A70 (Cumnock–Ayr)
6 A952 (A90 Birness–A90 Loomay)
7 A85 (A82–Oban)

WEATHER

- The windiest places in Scotland are the north-west coastal regions, the Orkneys, Shetland and the Western Isles.
- The highest air temperature recorded in Scotland was 32.9 degrees Celsius at Greycrook in the Borders on 9th August 2003.
- The lowest air temperature recorded in Scotland was also a record for the United Kingdom. A temperature of –27.2 degrees Celsius was recorded on three different occasions – at Braemar, Grampian, on the 11th February, 1895 and 10th January, 1982, and at Altnaharra, Highland Region, on 30th December 1995.
- The region with the highest mean annual temperature in Scotland is Dumfries and Galloway – approximately 9 degrees Celsius.
- The summit of Ben Nevis has the lowest mean annual temperature – approximately – 0.3 degrees Celsius.
- The most rain to fall in a thirty-minute period in the United Kingdom was recorded at Eskdalemuir, in Dumfries and Galloway. On 26th June, 1953, a total of 80mm rain fell in half an hour.

- The most rain to fall in a day was recorded at Sloy Main Adit, Loch Lomond. On 17th January, 1974, 238mm of rain fell in a period of twenty-four hours.
- The highest gust at high level was recorded at the Cairngorm Automatic Weather Station, which stands at an altitude of 1245m. On 20th March, 1986, a gust was recorded that reached a speed of 150 knots – 173 miles per hour.
- The highest gust at low level was recorded at Fraserburgh, Aberdeenshire, on 13th February, 1989. The speed of the gust was measured at 123 knots – 142 miles per hour.

WILDLIFE EXTREMES

- Biggest Atlantic salmon caught by line: Caught by Georgina Ballantyne in the River Tay, 1922. It weighed 64lbs/29kg.
- Biggest Atlantic salmon caught in a net: Caught in the 1890's in the River Tay. It weighed approximately 70lb/32kg.
- Biggest freshwater pearl found in Scotland: The Abernethy Pearl ('Wee Willie'), found in the River Tay in 1967, weighing 44g.
- Rarest plant in Scotland: The sticky catchfly (*lychnis viscaria*)
- Oldest tree in Scotland: The Fortingall Yew, near Aberfeldy. It is believed to be the oldest living thing in Europe.
- The rarest tree in Scotland: A sub-species of whitebeam, found only on the Isle of Arran.
- The tallest tree in Scotland: The position is hotly contested between three trees, all Douglas firs – 'Dughall Mor' (Big Dougal), in Reelig Glen Wood, Moniack, is currently acknowledged as the tallest. The other two trees can be found at Ardkinglass, Loch Fyne, and at Dunans Estate in Argyll.
- Scotland's rarest bird: A chough (type of crow), already extinct south of the Border.
- Scotland's rarest bird of prey: white-tailed sea eagle.
- Scotland's biggest bird of prey: white-tailed sea eagle.
- Scotland's smallest bird of prey: merlin falcon.
- Scotland's largest seabird: gannet.
- Scotland's smallest seabird: storm petrel.
- Largest gannet rookery in the world: St Kilda.
- Largest population of mammals native to Scotland: red deer.
- Largest land mammal of Scotland: red deer.
- Smallest land mammal in Scotland: harvest mouse (endangered species)

POLITICS

- The Scottish Office was created in 1884. In 1892 the Secretary for Scotland was given a seat on the cabinet. The title of Secretary for Scotland was changed to Secretary of State for Scotland in 1929. In 1939, the headquarters of the Scottish Office moved to St Andrews House in Edinburgh. In 1999, following devolution, most of the functions of the Scottish Office were transferred to the Scottish Executive and the Scottish Office was renamed the Scotland Office. In 2003, The Scotland Office was closed down.

- The first Labour candidate in a parliamentary election was a Scot, Keir Hardie (1856–1915). Originally a member of the Scottish Labour Party, Hardie founded the Independent Labour Party, which was to become the Labour Party, in 1893.

- The National Party of Scotland was founded in 1928. Through a merger with The Scottish Party in 1934 this became the Scottish National Party.

- The first woman to address the House of Lords was a Scot, Chrystal Macmillan (1882–1937). Chrystal Macmillan, one of the first female graduates from Edinburgh University, where she studied law, was a committed pacifist and a leading figure in the Women's Suffrage movement. In 1908 she addressed the House of Lords to argue the case for suffrage for female graduates.

- The first woman to become a Conservative minister was a Scot, Katharine Marjory Stewart-Murray, Duchess of Atholl (1874–1960). She served as Parliamentary Secretary to the Board of Education from 1924–29.

- The first leader (First Minister) of the devolved Scottish Parliament in 1999 was Donald Dewar.

ELECTION SYSTEM
FOR THE SCOTTISH PARLIAMENT

- There are 129 Members of the Scottish Parliament (MSPs).

- 73 MSPs are elected by the traditional 'first-past-the-post' system. Electors have one 'first-past-the post' vote, to make their choice of an individual from any party to represent their constituency. The candidate with the most votes in each constituency is elected.

- The remaining 56 MSPs are elected by the 'additional members system'. The 'additional members system' is a form of proportional representation. Scotland is divided into eight regions, each of which consists of eight to ten constituencies, and each of which has seven seats to be filled. Parties are invited to put forward a list of candidates, in order of preference, whom they have chosen to stand as additional members. Electors have a second vote, voting for a party in their region, rather than an individual. The votes are counted up and adjusted according to the number of seats each party has gained in the 'first-past-the-post' system. A party that has gained a great number of seats in the 'first-past-the-post' vote will be less likely to have many additional members. If a party is allocated one seat by the 'additional members system', the first candidate on the party list will fill the seat; if two seats have been awarded, the first two candidates will fill them, and so on.

- If an MSP voted into the Scottish Parliament by the 'first-past-the-post' system dies or resigns, a by-election must take place to fill his or her seat. If an MSP voted in by the 'additional members' system dies or resigns, the seat is filled by the next member on the party list.

THE FATHER OF –

Donald Dewar	The Father of Devolution
Adam Ferguson	The Father of Sociology
Niel Gow	The Father of Strathspey and Reel Music
Thomas Graham	The Father of Colloidal Chemistry
Samuel Greig	The Father of the Russian Navy
James Hutton	The Father of Modern Geology
William Hunter	The Father of Scientific Surgery
John Paul Jones	The Father of the American Navy
Lachlan Macquarie	The Father of Australia
John Muir	The Father of the Environmental Movement
Sir Walter Scott	The Father of Historical Fiction
Adam Smith	The Father of Economics

APPELLATIONS OF SOME FAMOUS SCOTS

Robert Burns, poet – The Ploughman Poet
Billy Connolly, comedian – The Big Yin
Lonnie Donegan, musician – The King of Skiffle
Thomas Blake Glover, – The Scottish Samurai
industrial pioneer in Japan
John Graham, Viscount Claverhouse, – Bonnie Dundee, Bluidy Clavers
Jacobite leader

James Hogg, poet	— The Ettrick Shepherd
James Crichton, intellectual star of the Scottish Enlightenment	— The Admirable Crichton
Sir George Mackenzie of Rosehaugh, seventeenth century lawyer, prominent in the prosecution of Scottish Covenanters	— Bluidy Mackenzie
William Miller, poet	— The Laureate of the Nursery
Chic Murray, comedian	— The Tall Droll
Michael Scott, scholar	— The Wondrous Wizard
Sir Walter Scott, poet and novelist	— The Wizard of the North, The Bold Buccleugh, The Great Unknown

QUOTATIONS FROM FAMOUS SCOTS

Sir J(ames) M(atthew) Barrie, 1860–1937, playwright and novelist
To die will be an awfully big adventure.

Peter Pan (1904)

Alexander Graham Bell, 1847–1922 teacher and inventor
Mr Watson, come here; I want you.

First words spoken by telephone (attrib) (1876)

Robert the Bruce, 1274–1329, king of Scotland
Now, God be with you my dear children. I have breakfasted with you and shall sup with my lord Jesus Christ.

Last words (attributed)

Robert Burns, 1759–1796, poet and songwriter
The rank is but a guinea's stamp,
The man's the gowd for a' that;
For a' that and a' that
A man's a man for a' that.

For A' That and A' That (1790)

Thomas Carlyle, 1795–1881, historian
History is a distillation of rumour.

The French Revolution 1837

Andrew Carnegie, 1835–1919, Scots-born American industrialist
No man will make a great leader who wants to do it all himself, or to get all the credit for doing it.

Sir Arthur Conan Doyle, 1859–1930, physician and writer
It is an old maxim of mine that when you have excluded the impossible, whatever remains, however improbable, must be the truth.

The Sign of Four (1894)

Sir David Hume, 1711–1776, philosopher and historian
Be a philosopher; but, amidst all your philosophy, be still a man.

A Treatise of Human Nature (1739-40)

James V, 1512–1542, king of Scotland
Adieu, farewell, it cam' wi' a lass, it will pass wi' a lass.

Dying words

James VI and I, 1566–1625, king of Scotland and England
No Bishop, no King.

John Knox, 1513–72, religious reformer
A man with God is always in the majority.

R D Laing, 1927–89, psychiatrist
No one *has* schizophrenia, like having a cold. The patient has not 'got' schizophrenia. He is schizophrenic.

The Divided Self (1965)

Mary, Queen of Scots, 1542–87
In my end is my beginning.

James Graham, Marquis of Montrose 1612–50, Scottish General
He either fears his fate too much,
Or his deserts are small,
That puts it not unto the touch
To win or lose them all.

My Dear and Only Love (1642)

Chic Murray, 1919–1985, comedian
You know what they say about stamp collecting – philately will get you nowhere.

Sir Walter Scott, 1771–1832, Scottish novelist and poet
And come he slow, or come he fast,
It is but Death who comes at last.

Marmion (1808)

Robert Louis Balfour Stevenson, 1850–94, novelist and poet
Wealth I seek not; hope nor love,
Nor a friend to know me;
All I seek, the heaven above
And the road below me.

The Vagabond 1895

QUOTATIONS ON SCOTLAND AND THE SCOTS

Sir J(ames) M(atthew) Barrie, 1860–1937, Scottish playwright and novelist
You've forgotten the grandest moral attribute of a Scotsman, Maggie, that he'll do nothing which might damage his career.

What Every Woman Knows, Act I (1908)

Samuel Johnson, 1709–1784, English writer and critic
Much may be made of a Scotchman, if he be caught young.

Seeing Scotland, Madam, is only seeing a worse England. It is seeing the flower fade away to the naked stalk.

Samuel Johnson: quoted in James Boswell's *Life of Samuel Johnson* (1791)

Alasdair James Gray, 1934– , Scottish novelist, painter and playwright
Glasgow, the sort of industrial city where most people live nowadays but nobody imagines living.

Lanark (1981)

(Frederic) Ogden Nash, 1902–1971, American humorist
No MacTavish
Was ever lavish

Genealogical Reflection (1931)

William Somerset Maugham, 1874–1965, English writer
Scotchmen seem to think it's a credit to them to be Scotch.

A Writer's Notebook (1949)

Sir Walter Scott, 1771–1832, Scottish novelist and poet
O Caledonia! Stern and wild,
Meet nurse for a poetic child!
Land of brown heath and shaggy wood,
Land of the mountain and the flood,
Land of my sires! What mortal hand
Can e'er untie the filial band,
That knits me to thy rugged strand!

The Lay of the Last Minstrel (1805)

Tobias George Smollett, 1721–1771, Scottish novelist
The Scots have a slight tincture of letters, with which they make a parade
among people who are more illiterate than themselves; but they may be said
to float on the surface of science, and they have made every small advances
in the useful arts.

Humphrey Clinker (1771)

Voltaire (Francois Marie Arouet), 1694–1778, French writer
We look to Scotland for all our ideas of civilisation.

**(Thomas) Woodrow Wilson, 1856–1924, twenty-eighth President of the
   USA**
Every line of strength in American history is a line coloured with Scottish
blood.

**Sir P(elham) G(renville) Wodehouse, 1881–1975 English humorous
   writer**
It is never difficult to distinguish between a Scotsman with a grievance and
a ray of sunshine.

Blandings Castle and Elsewhere (1935)

HORSE RACING IN SCOTLAND

- Horse racing has been a popular sport in Scotland for several hundred years. James IV enjoyed the sport. Horse races were originally local events, and were often a part of festivities on fairs, festivals and other special occasions in various parts of the country. One of the oldest racing events in Scotland was the Lanark Silver Bell, which is thought to date from the early seventeenth century. The race no longer takes place as Lanark Racecourse was forced to close as a major racing venue in 1977.
- Ayr Racecourse. Founded 1907. Home to the Scottish Grand National (April) and the Ayr Gold Cup (September).
- Hamilton Park Racecourse. Founded in 1888. Famous for its annual 'Saints and Sinners' event, held in June.
- Kelso Racecourse. Founded 1822. Hurdle, steeplechase and flat racing events. Host to the Buccleuch Cup (April).
- Musselburgh Racecourse, near Edinburgh. Founded 1816. 27 racing days a year.
- Perth Racecourse. Founded 1613. Host to the City of Perth Gold Cup. Races at Perth were originally held on the North Inch.

PRESBYTERIAN TIMEKEEPING
Did you know ... ?

A clockmaker from Pittenweem once made a clock with four dials. The clock showed the minutes, hours, days of the week and months of the year. It also chimed – but never on the Sabbath!

PRIME MINISTERS OF GREAT BRITAIN WHO WERE BORN IN SCOTLAND

1762–3	John Stuart, 3rd Earl of Bute
1852–55	George Hamilton Gordon, 4th Earl of Aberdeen
1894–95	Archibald Philip Primrose, 5th Earl of Rosebery
1902–5	Arthur James Balfour, 1st Earl of Balfour

1905–8	Sir Henry Campbell-Bannerman
1922–23	Andrew Bonar Law
1924, 1929–35	James Ramsay MacDonald
1963–64	Alexander Frederick Douglas-Home, 14th Earl of Home
1997–2007	Anthony Charles Lynton Blair
2007–	James Gordon Brown

RIVERS

- The longest river in Scotland is the River Tay, which is approximately 120 miles long.
- The Spey, approximately 110 miles long, is the second longest river.
- The lengths of Scotland's other major rivers, in descending order, are as follows:

  The River Clyde – 106 miles

  The River Tweed – 97 miles

  The River Dee – 85 miles

  The River Don – 82 miles

  The River Forth – 65 miles
- The River Tay is recognised as one of the best salmon fishing rivers in Scotland and it has been on the Tay that catches of salmon of record-breaking weights, either caught by line or by net, have been made.
- The area around the River Spey is famous for its many distilleries. The waters of the river are an essential ingredient in the whisky making process.
- The River Clyde became famous as an international centre for shipbuilding in the nineteenth century. When the Cunard liner the Queen Elizabeth, built at John Brown's shipyard on the Clyde, was launched in 1938, she was the biggest passenger liner ever built.
- The area around the Falls of Clyde at New Lanark is now a Wildlife Reserve.

FORTH BRIDGE FACTS AND FIGURES

- The original designer of the Forth Bridge was Thomas Bouch, but his rail bridge across the Tay collapsed on December 28th 1879 and Sir John Fowler and Benjamin Baker were appointed instead.
- The main contractor was William Arrol
- Construction began in 1883.
- At it's height, the number of people employed in the construction reached 4,600.

- The bridge consists of 55,00 tons of steel, 640,000 cubic feet of Aberdeen granite and over 8,000,000 rivets. The last rivet was driven home in a ceremony on March 4th 1890 by the Prince of Wales (later Edward VII). This last rivet was made of gold.
- The total cost of construction came to £3.2 million.
- 145 acres of paint were used to coat the bridge. The paint is manufactured especially for the bridge by Craig & Rose of Leith, Edinburgh and contrary to popular belief, workers do not start at one end of the bridge and paint to the other end before starting all over again. They paint the bridge in sections depending on where it is needed most at any one time.
- From mid-winter to mid-summer the bridge expands by almost 1 metre.
- Overall length: 8296 feet (2528.7 metres)
- South approach: 10 spans of 168 ft (51.2m)
- North approach: 5 spans of 168 ft (5.12m)
- Length portal to portal: 5350 ft (1630.7m)
- Length from tower to tower: 1912 ft (582.8m)
- Cantilever length: 680 ft (207.3m)
- Main spans:1710 ft (521.3m)
- Height of towers: 330 ft (100.6m)
- Weight of 1710 ft. span: 11571 tons (11754 tonnes)
- Number of rivets: 6,500,000
- Weight of rivets: 4200 tons (4267 tonnes)
- Total cost: £3.2m

TEN LONGEST BRIDGES IN SCOTLAND

Tay Railway Bridge	3135m
Forth Bridge	2528m
Tay Road Bridge	2253m
Forth Road Bridge	1828m
Kessock Bridge	1052m
Erskine Bridge	660m
Skye Bridge	570m
Clava Viaduct	549m
Findhorn Viaduct	400m
North Bridge	346m

SCOTTISH PHILANTHROPISTS

A small list to debunk the myth that all Scots are mean.

Andrew Bell
(1753–1832) Fife-born teacher. Pioneered what became known as the Madras system of education when he was working in India and brought it back to this country where it was widely adopted. Paid for the founding of two schools using his teaching methods – Madras College in St Andrews, and Madras Academy (later re-named Bell Baxter High School) in Cupar.

Andrew Carnegie
(1835–1919) Dunfermline-born American industrialist. Donated more than £70,000,000 for libraries and arts and education institutions in the US and Great Britain.

David Dale
(1739–1806) Industrialist. Established the cotton mills at New Lanark, providing the workers with humane working conditions, medical care and education for the children. He also employed and educated hundreds of poor children from the city of Glasgow.

James Donaldson
(1751–1830) newspaper proprietor. Bequeathed money for the founding of Donaldson's Hospital in Edinburgh.

Mary Erskine
(1629–1707) Edinburgh businesswoman and banker. Donated a large sum of money to the Company of Edinburgh Merchants for the founding of a school for girls (1694).

James Gillespie
(1726–97) snuff merchant. Bequeathed money for the founding of James Gillespie's School.

Robert Gordon
(1688–1731) Aberdeen-born merchant. Retired to Aberdeen after making his fortune trading in Poland. Left his entire estate for the founding of a residential school for boys – the Robert Gordon Hospital (1750).

George Hutcheson
(1580–1639) and Thomas Hutcheson, (1589–1641), brothers, both Glasgow lawyers. Provided money for the founding of the Hutcheson Hospital for poor men and boys, which later became the Hutcheson Grammar School.

George Heriot
(1563–1624) goldsmith to King James VI. Bequeathed money for the founding of George Heriot's School.

CURLING MISCELLANY

The sport of curling is said to have originated in Scotland, probably around the fifteenth century. The long, cold Scottish winters provided many stretches of deep-frozen water on which participants could practise. The earliest curling club recorded was in Kilsyth, in the early sixteenth century. An annual bonspiel, a curling competition, was held for many years at the Lake of Menteith in Perthshire, attracting competitors from all over Scotland. Nowadays, curling is played on indoor ice rinks. The international governing body for the sport, the World Curling Federation, is based in Edinburgh. The Royal Caledonian Curling Club of Scotland serves as the parent body to hundreds of clubs worldwide. In spite of curling's Scottish origins, it has in recent times become one of the poor relations of sport in Scotland. However, national interest in curling was revived by the success of the British women's curling team, all of whom were Scots, at the 2002 Winter Olympics in Salt Lake City.

Curling stones are traditionally made from Ailsa Craig granite and weigh around 42 lbs. Curling teams consist of four players. The rules are very similar to those of bowls. The rink, or sheet, on which the game is played, measures 146ft by 15ft (approx).

CURLING TERMINOLOGY

Back Line: Line across the rink at the back edge of the house, marking point beyond which a stone is considered out of play.

Biter: Stone just touching outside circle of house.

Bonspiel: A curling tournament with events for several teams.

Centre Line: Line running down the centre of the rink from end to end.

Chip and Lie: A stone striking another stone and stopping while still in play.

Counter: A stone lying in the house closer to the centre than the opponent's stones.

Curl: The sideways swing of a stone as it travels, achieved by twisting the handle of the stone on delivery.

Draw: A stone that reaches the house.

End: When all four players in each team deliver two curling stones each from one end of the rink to the other. There are 8-10 ends in every game.

Guard: A stone placed in front of another one to protect it from being knocked out of play, or placed in front of the house to hinder the other team.

Hacks: Rubber-coated footholds built into the ice at the end of the rink, from where the curling stones are delivered.

Hammer: The last stone to be delivered in an end.

Hog: A stone that does not travel beyond the hog line and must be removed from play.

Hog Line: Lines across the rink twenty-one feet from the tee line. Players must release their curling stone before the first hog line and it must travel beyond the second.

House: The circle, twelve feet in diameter, within which a stone may score.

Keen Ice: Where the condition of the ice means there is less friction and stones travel further with less effort.

Lead: Player who plays the first two stones for the team.

Rock: A curling stone

Skip: The captain of a curling team – often the last to play in each end.

Sweeping: Brushing the ice in front of a moving stone to smooth its passage, helping it to travel further and guiding it in a particular direction.

Take-out: Removal of an opponent's stone from play by striking it with your own stone.

Tee: The centre spot in the middle of the house.

Touched running stone: A stone touched while moving by foot or broom. (In most circumstances, it will have to be removed from play). Sometimes referred to as a 'burned stone'.

CURLING VENUES AROUND SCOTLAND

Aberdeen Ice Rink (The Ice Rink Club)

Atholl Ice Rink (Atholl Curling Rink Ltd)

Ayr Ice Rink (Ayrshire Curlers)

Border Ice Rink, Kelso

Braehead Ice Rink (Braehead Curling)

Brora Ice Rink

Drimsynie Leisure Centre, Lochgoilhead

Dundee Ice Arena

Dumfries Ice Bowl

Elgin Leisure Centre

Forest Hills, Aberfoyle

Forfar Ice Rink

The Galleon Centre, Kilmarnock

Gogar Park, Edinburgh (Gogar Park Curling Club)

Greenacres Curling Rink, Renfrewshire

Green Hotel, Kinross

Harvies (Stevenson)
Inverness Ice Centre
Fife Ice Arena (Kirkcaldy Curling Club)
Laggon Leisure Centre, Paisley
Lanarkshire Ice Rink, Hamilton
Letham Grange Resort
Lockerbie Ice Rink
Murrayfield Ice Rink, Edinburgh
Perth Ice Rink, Dewar's Centre, Perth
Stirling Ice Rink
Waterfront Ice Rink, Waterfront Leisure Complex

SHINTY

Shinty – or camanachd, as it is properly known – is claimed to be the oldest sport in Scotland. It is thought to have originated in Ireland, where they play a similar game, called Hurling. Shinty is a bit like a cross between hockey and lacrosse. Players play with a caman, not unlike a hockey stick. They are permitted to swing the caman as high as they please, o hit the ball with either side of the caman, and to stop the ball using their feet, but they are not allowed to touch it with their hands. The ball is leather-covered, and stuffed with cork and worsted. Shinty games are played between two teams of twelve players and last ninety minutes. The game demands considerable stamina, agility and courage. The earliest records of rules for shinty date from 1861, set down by the Aberdeen University Shinty Club. In 1870, The Society of True Highlanders published a history of the game and a detailed set of rules in The Book of the Society of the True Gael. The Glasgow Celtic Society formalised the game by distributing a set of rules of play to a number of lowland clubs in Scotland in 1879 – the Highland clubs took a little longer to organise themselves, but in 1880, Strathglass Shinty Club produced a set of rules and regulations and a constitution – the first Highland club to do so. The Glasgow Celtic Society Cup, the oldest competition in shinty, was set up in 1879. The Camanachd Association was set up in 1894, and published a full set of revised rules for all associated clubs.

SHINTY CLUBS IN SCOTLAND

Aberdeen University
Ballachulish

Beauly
Boleskine

Bute
Caberfeidh
Col Glen
Dunfermline
Edinburgh East Lothian
Edinburgh University
Fort William
Glasgow Mid Argyll
Glasgow University
Glangarry
Glenorchy
Glen Urquhart
The Highlanders
Inveraly
Inverness
Kilmallie
Kilmory
Kincraig

Kingussie
Kinlochshiel
Kintyre
Kyles Athletic
Lochaber Camanachd
Loch Broom
London
Lovat
Newtonmore
Oban Camanachd
Oban Celtic
Skye Camanachd
St Andrews University
Strachur
Strathclyde Police
Strachglass
Tayforth
Taynuilt

GOLF MISCELLANY

Scotland is the birthplace of golf and the game has been played here for many centuries. The earliest documented evidence of the game dates back to the reign of James II, when the wrath of the parliament came down upon both football and golf and an attempt was made to ban both sports in favour of more military pursuits, such as archery – to no avail, it would seem. The game continued to be popular, even with royalty. James IV, James V and James VI all played. During the Reformation, the Kirk elders railed against golf on the Sabbath – but still it was played. Although it was still some time before golfing societies came into existence, some of the places where golf is still played to this day – notably St Andrews 'The Home of Golf' – were popular with lovers of the sport almost four hundred years ago.

THE FIRST GOLFING SOCIETIES IN SCOTLAND

The Royal Burgess Golf Society, Edinburgh: Founded 1735.
The Honourable Company of Edinburgh Golfers: Founded 1744.

The Royal and Ancient Golf Club of St Andrews: Founded 1754.
The Bruntsfield Links Golfing Society: Founded 1761.
The Royal Musselburgh Golf Club: Founded 1774.
The Royal Aberdeen Golf Club: Founded 1780.
The Crail Golfing Society: Founded 1786.
The Glasgow Golf Club: Founded 1787.
The Burntisland Golf Club: Founded 1791.

THE OPEN GOLF CHAMPIONSHIP

- St Andrews hosted the first Open Championship in 1860 and since then has hosted the competition more often than any other British venue (26 times, 1860–2003). Prestwick comes a close second (24 times) and Muirfield, Gullane, third (15 times).
- The largest margin of victory in the Open Championship – 13 strokes – was achieved by a Scot, 'Old' Tom Morris (1821–1908) in 1862. His son, 'Young' Tom Morris (1851–1875) almost equalled his father's record, winning the Open of 1870 by a margin of twelve strokes.
- 'Young' Tom Morris won the Open four times in succession, in 1868, 1869, 1870 and 1872 (there was no Open Championship in 1871). His father won twice in succession, in 1861 an 1862.
- 'Old' Tom Morris holds the record for the oldest winner in the Open Championship. He was 46 years, 3 months and 7 days old when he won it in 1868.
- 'Young' Tom Morris became the youngest ever winner of the Open Championship when he won in 1868, aged 17 years, 5 months and 8 days. Young Tom also holds the record for the youngest competitor – he was only 14 years, 4 months and 4 days old when he played in his first Open in 1865.
- Another Scot, William Auchterlonie, was the second youngest winner when he won in 1893, aged 21 years, 3 months and 12 days.

HOLES AT THE OLD COURSE ST ANDREWS

Hole	Name	Medal	Ladies
1	Burn	370 par 4	399 par 4
2	Dyke	411 par 4	375 par 5
3	Cartgate (out)	352 par 4	321 par 4

Hole	Name	Medal	Ladies
4	Ginger Beer	419 par 4	401 par 5
5	Hole O'Cross (Out)	514 par 5	454 par 5
6	Heathery (Out)	374 par 4	325 par 4
7	High (out)	359 par 4	335 par 4
8	Short	166 par 3	145 par 3
9	End	307 par 4	261 par 4
10	Bobby Jones	318 par 4	296 par 4
11	High (In)	173 par 3	150 par 3
12	Heathery (In)	316 par 4	304 par 4
13	Hole O'Cross (In)	398 par 4	377 par 5
14	Long	523 par 5	487 par 5
15	Cartgate (In)	414 par 4	369 par 4
16	Corner of the Dyke	381 par 4	325 par 4
17	Road	461 par 4	426 par 5
18	Tom Morris	354 par 4	342 par 4

RULES OF GOLF 1744

The Royal and Ancient Golf Club of St Andrews governs and has copyright of the modern rules of golf. The following are the earliest surviving written rules of golf, compiled by the Gentlemen Golfers of Leith, later the honourable company of Edinburgh golfers, 7th March 1744.

Articles and Laws in Playing at Golf, 1744

1 You must tee your ball within a club's length of the hole.

2 Your tee must be on the ground.

3 You are not to change the ball which you strike off the tee.

4 You are not to remove stones, bones or any break club for the sake of playing your ball, except upon the fair green, and that only within a club's length of the ball.

5 If your ball comes among watter, or any wattery filth, you are at liberty to take out your ball and bringing it behind the hazard and teeing it, you may play it with any club and allow your adversary a stroke for so getting out your ball.

6 If your balls be found anywhere touching one another you are to lift the first ball till you play the last.

7 At holing you are to play your ball honestly at the hole, and not to play upon your adversary's ball, not lying in your way to the hole.

8 If you should lose your ball, by its being taken up, or any other way, you are to go back to the spot where you struck last and drop another ball and allow your adversary a stroke for the misfortune.

9 No man at holing his ball is to be allowed to mark his way to the hole with his club or anything else.

10 If a ball be stopp'd by any person, horse, dog, or any thing else, the ball so stopp'd must be played where it lyes.

11 If you draw your club in order to strike and proceed so far in the stroke as to be bringing down your club, if then your club should break in any way, it is to be accounted a stroke.

12 He whose ball lyes farthest from the hole is obliged to play first.

13 Neither trench, ditch, or dyke made for the preservation of the links, nor the Scholar's Holes or the soldier's lines shall be accounted a hazard but the ball is to be taken out, teed and play'd with any iron club.

SCOTLAND ROCKS
Did you know ... ?

The oldest rock in Britain is Lewisian Gneiss, which forms the bedrock of much of the northern coastal regions of mainland of Scotland, the islands of the Hebrides and Orkney and Shetland. It is a hard metamorphic rock, formed from igneous rocks which have been subjected to extremely high pressure and intense heat and is more than 3000 million years old.

SCOTS GLOSSARY

ae: one, the same
aft: often
aye: always
amaist: almost
bairn: child

bawbee: a halfpenny
ben the hoose: inside
brae: slope, hill
braw: very good, fine
breeks: breeches, trousers

but and ben: a two-roomed house

clabby-dhu: a mussel

corbie: a crow

crouse: perky, bright and cheerful

cuddy: a donkey, or horse

cundy: a covered drain

darg: a day's work

dicht/dight: to wipe

dook: to duck, to bathe

dree: to suffer, endure

dreich: dreary

ee: eye

ettle: to aim, to intend

fecht: fight

fit: foot

fouter about: to mess around, or indulge in fruitless activity

gae: to go

gang: to go

gie: to give

glaikit: foolish

glaur: mud, marsh, mire

glen: valley

gloaming: twilight

gowan: a daisy

gowd: gold

gowf: golf

gowk: a fool

gowpen: a double handful, i.e. as much as can be held in two hands.

greet: to cry

hantle: a good amount

heid: head

hurdies: buttocks, thighs

ilk'a: each, every

jaup: to splash

Jenny-long-legs: a crane-fly

keek: to peep

keeker: a black eye

ken: to know

kyte: belly

loon: a boy (NE Scotland)

maun: must

midden: a refuse/compost heap.

misken: to ignore, overlook, fail to recognise, snub

mou: mouth

muckle: great, much, big

nieve: fist

nit: nut

onie: any

painch: paunch

peely-wally: pale and unwell

peevers: hopscotch

peerie: a top

plack: an old Scots coin of very little value

pleuch: plough

pock: pouch, bag

queyn, or quine: a girl (NE Scotland)

rash: rush

rive: belch

sauf: to save

scaff: ne'er do well, riff-raff

sconner/scunner: disgust

sea-maw: gull

semmit: a vest

shoogle: to shake, or swing

sic: such

skail: to spill, scatter

skelf: a splinter

skinking: watery

slaver: to dribble saliva from the mouth

sleekit: sly, cunning

sned: to cut off

staw: to sicken

stoochie: disturbance, fuss

swall'd: swollen
tattie bogle: a scarecrow
tint: lost
thairm: guts, intestines
thrissle: thistle
tup: ram
wabbit: tired, worn-out

waukrife: wakeful
wean: a small child
weel-kent: familiar, well-known
wether: sheep
whiles: sometimes
wordy: worthy
yird: earth

SCOTTISH PROVERBS AND SAYINGS

A burnt bairn dreads the fire.

A deaf man will hear the clink o' money.

Aft ettle, whiles hit.

A hook is weel tint to catch a salmon.

'Amaist' and 'very near' have aye been great liars.

An auld pock is aye skailing.

Ane's own hearth is gowd's worth.

Before ye mak' a friend, eat a peck o' salt wi' him.

Better unborn than untaught.

Buy what ye dinna want and you'll sell what ye canna spare.

Ding down the nests and the rooks will flee away.

Gude folk are scarce, tak' care o' ane.

Hold your hands off other folk's bairns, till ye get some o' yer ain.

I canna sell the cow and hae the milk.

If it's for ye, it'll not go by ye.

If marriages be made in heaven, some had few friends there.

If ye be not ill, be not ill-like.

Ilka doorstep has its ain slippery stane.

Ill bairns are aye best heard at hame.

Keep something for a sair fit.

Keep yer ain fish-guts tae yer ain sea-maws.

Muckle heid, little wit.

Ne'er scald yer lips in other fowk's kail.

Placks and bawbees grow pounds.

Poor fowk's freends soon misken them.

Reckless youth makes youthful age.

Shame fa' them that shame think tae dae themselves a gude turn.

Sic as ye gie sic ye will get.

Snotty folks are sweet, but slavering folks are weet.

Some hae a hantle fauts, ye're only a ne'er-do-weel.

The de'il and the dean begin with wi' ae letter; when the de'il has the dean, the kirk will be the better.

The first thing a poor gentleman calls for in the morning is a needle and thread.

Were it not for hope the heart would break.

What ye dae when ye are drunk ye maun pay for when ye are sober.

Whaur there's a Jock there's a Jenny.

SCOTTISH TOWN AND CITY MOTTOES

Aberdeen	Bon Accord
Crail	In Verbo Tuo Laxabo Rete (At Thy Word I Will Let Down the Net)
Dundee	Dei Donum Prudentia et Candore (Gift of God with Thought and Purity)
Edinburgh	Nisi Dominus Frustra (Except the Lord in Vain)
Elie and Earlsferry	Unitas Alit Comitatem (Unity Fosters Courtesy)
Eyemouth	Remis Velisque (With Oars and Sails)
Galashiels	Sour Plums
Glasgow	Lord Let Glasgow Flourish
Inverness	A Hundred Thousand Welcomes
Jedburgh	Strenue et Prospere (Earnestly and Successfully)
Kelso	Dae Richt – Fear Nocht
Kirkcaldy	Vigilando Munio (They Stand Guard)
Melrose	One Community Open to All
Montrose	Mare Ditat Rosa Decorat (The Sea Enriches, The Rose Adorns)
Peebles	Contra Nando Incrementum (Increase by Swimming Against the Flood)
Perth	Make Haste Slowly
St Andrews	Dum Spiro Spero (While I Breathe I Hope)
St Monans	Mare Vivimus (By the Sea We Live)
Stirling	The Britons stand by the force of arms
	The Scots are by this cross preserved from harms
	The Castle and Bridge of Stirling town
	Are in the compass of this seal set down.

SCOTTISH PLACENAMES ABROAD

Aberdeen, Maryland, USA

Aberdeen, Mississipi, USA

Aberdeen, New South Wales, Australia

Aberdeen, Saskatchewan, Canada

Aberdeen, South Dakota, USA

Aberdeen, Washington, USA

Aberdeen, Hong Kong, China

Aberdeen, South Africa

Aberdeen Lake, North West Territories,
  Canada

Arnprior, Canada

Ayr, Queensland, Australia

Blair Athol, Queensland, Australia

Callander, Ontario, Canada

Clyde, Alberta, Canada

Clyde, New York, USA

Clyde, Ohio, USA

Clyde, New Zealand

Clyde River, Nortyh West Territories, Canada

Crawford, Nebraska, USA

Douglas, Alaska

Douglas, Arizona

Douglas, Georgia

Douglas, Wyoming

Douglas, South Africa

Dunbar, Queensland, Australia

Dundee, Michigan, USA

Dundee, New York, USA

Dundee, South Africa

Edinburgh, Indiana, USA

Edinburg, Texas, USA

Edinburg, Illinois, USA

Elgin, Illinois, USA

Elgin, North Dakota, USA

Elgin, Nevada, USA

Elgin, Utah, USA

Elgin Down, Queensland, Australia

Fife Lake, Michigan, USA
Glasgow, Kentucky, USA
Glasgow, Montana, USA
Glasgow, Virginia USA
Glasgow, Jamaica
New Glasgow, Nova Scotia, Canada
Glencoe, Ontario, Canada
Glencoe, South Africa
Glengarry Range, Western Australia
Gordon Bay, Melville Island, Northern
   Territory, Australia
Gordon Downs, Western Australia
Lake Gordon, Tasmania, Australia
Gordon Lake, North West Territories, Canada
Gordon River, Tasmania, Australia
Huntly, New Zealand
Inverness, Florida, USA
Inverness, Nova Scotia, Canada
Iona, Angola
Irvine, California, USA
Irvine, Kentucky, USA
Kelso, California, ISA
Kelso, Washington, USA
Kincardine, Ontario, Canada
Kinross, South Africa
Lanark, Illinois, USA
Lanark, Ontario, Canada
Livingston, California, USA
Livingston, Montana, USA
Livingston, Tennessee, USA
Livingston, Texas, USA
Livingston Mountains. New Zealand
Montrose, Colorado, USA
Montrose, Michigan, USA
Montrose, Pennsylvania, USA
Oban, Nigeria
Perth, Ontario, Canada
Perth, Tasmania, Australia
Perth, Western Australia

Scotland, Ontario, Canada
Selkirk Mountains, British Columbia, Canada
St Andrews, New Brunswick, Canada
Stirling, South Australia
Stirling, City, California, USA
Mount Stirling, Western Australia
Strathmore, Alberta, Canada
Strathnaver, British Columbia, Canada
Sutherland, Nebraska, USA
Sutherland, South Africa
Thurso, Quebec, Canada

SCOTTISH PLACES ...
OTHERWISE KNOWN AS

Aberdeen	The Brave Toun
Anstruther	Anster
Ayr	Auld Ayr
Crail	Caryle
Dumfries	The Queen of the South
Dunblane	Drukken Dunblane
Dunfermline	The Auld Grey Toon
Edinburgh	Auld Reekie, or Athens of the North.
Elgin Cathedral	The Lantern of the North
Forfar	Brosie Forfar
St Mary's, Haddington	The Lanthorn o' the Lothians
Inverness	The Capital of the Highlands
Jedburgh	Jethart, The Gateway to Scotland
Kirkcaldy	The Lang Toun
Lanarkshire	The Orchard of Scotland
Langholm	The Muckle Toun
Lauder	Lousy Lauder
Linlithgow	The Faithfu' Toun
Livingston	The capital of Silicon Glen
Moray	The Granary of Scotland
Musselburgh	The Honest Toun
The National Monument,	Edinburgh's Shame, or
Calton Hill, Edinburgh	Scotland's Pride and Poverty, or
	Scotland's Disgrace

Oban	The Gateway to the Isles,
	The Charing Cross of Scotland
Peebles	Peebles for Pleasure
Perth	St John's Town, or the Fair City
Pitlochry	The Gateway to the Highlands
Scotland	Alba, Caledonia, Scotia,
	The Knuckle-end of England,
	Home of the Brave, Land of Song
St Andrews	The Home of Golf
Stewarton	The Bonnet Toun
Sleat	Russet Sleat of Beauteous Women

STATIONS ON THE CLOCKWORK ORANGE, GLASGOW'S SUBWAY

Opened in 1896, the Strathclyde Passenger Transport subway is the world's third oldest after London and Budapest. The Glasgow underground has only two lines, an outer (clockwise) and inner circle (anti-clockwise), stopping at all of the stations on the route, which are: St Enoch, Bridge Street, West Street, Shields Road, Kinning Park, Cessnock, Ibrox, Govan, Partick, Kelvinhall, Hillhead, Kelvinbridge, St George's Cross, Cowcaddens, Buchanan Street.

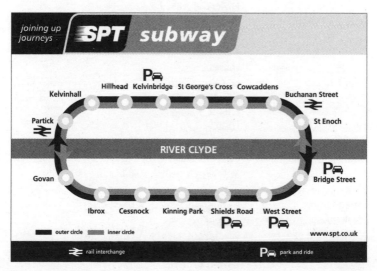

BURIAL PLACES OF FAMOUS SCOTS

Alexander III	Dunfermline Abbey
J M Barrie	Kirriemuir, Angus
John Balliol	Sweetheart Abbey, Dumfries
Robert the Bruce	Dunfermline Abbey (his heart was taken on crusade by his comrade Douglas and is now buried at Melrose Abbey)
Robert Burns	Dumfries
Thomas Carlyle	The churchyard, Ecclefechan
Andrew Carnegie	Sleepy Hollow, New York
Charles Edward Stuart (Bonnie Prince Charlie)	St Peter's, Rome
James II	Holyrood Abbey, Edinburgh
James III	Cambuskenneth Abbey, Stirlingshire
James IV	James IV's body was removed from Flodden Field and taken to London. It lay, embalmed but unburied in the Monastery of Sheen for several years. Following the dissolution of the monasteries it was consigned to a storage room. His body was eventually buried at an unknown location.
James V	Holyrood Abbey, Edinburgh
John Paul Jones	Originally buried in St Louis cemetery. His remains were moved in 1905 to Annapolis, where they were placed in the American Naval Academy chapel crypt.
John Knox	St Giles Churchyard (no longer in existence), Edinburgh. There is a monument to Knox in St Giles Cathedral.
David Livingstone	Westminster Abbey
Flora Macdonald	Kilmuir, Isle of Skye
William McGonagall	Pauper's grave, Greyfriars Kirkyard, Edinburgh
James Graham, Marquis of Montrose	St Giles Cathedral, Edinburgh
David Hume	Calton Hill cemetery, Edinburgh
Macbeth, king of Scots	Iona abbey
Mary, Queen of Scots	Chapel of Henry VII, Westminster Abbey (originally Peterborough – her remains were moved in 1612)

Sir Henry Raeburn	St John's Churchyard, Edinburgh
David Rizzio	Canongate Kirkyard
Robert III	Paisley Abbey
Rob Roy	Balquhidder
Michael Scott	Melrose Abbey
Sir Walter Scott	Dryburgh Abbey
Alexander Selkirk	At sea, off the coast of Africa
Mary Slessor	Duke Town, Calabar, Nigeria
Adam Smith	Canongate Kirkyard, Edinburgh
Robert Louis Stevenson	Mt Vaea, Samoa
Thomas Telford	Westminster Abbey
William Wallace	Wallace's arm is believed to have been buried by the monks of Cambuskenneth Abbey some months after his execution. The whereabouts of his other body parts are unknown.
James Watt	Handsworth Church, Middlesex.

FIRSTS AND LASTS FOR SCOTLAND

80 AD	The Romans under Agricola invaded Scotland for the first time.
208	The last Roman invasion of Caledonia took place, led by Septimus Severus.
430	The first Christian church in Scotland was established at Whithorn by St Ninian.
c.843	Kenneth MacAlpin became the first King of the Scots and Picts.
1099	Donald III became the last king of Scots to be buried on the island of Iona.
1250	Queen Margaret, wife of Malcolm III, was canonised, becoming Scotland's first (and only) royal saint.
1349	The first cases of the Black Death in Scotland.
1371	Robert II, first of the Stewart monarchs, came to the throne.
1383	Bishop Wardlaw of Glasgow is the first Scot to be made a cardinal.
1411	The first university in Scotland was founded at St Andrews.
1493	John Macdonald, the fourth Lord of the Isles became the last Lord of the Isles when James IV forfeited his lands.
1508	Walter Chepman and Andrew Myllar set up the first Scottish printing press, in Edinburgh.
1600	Charles I was born, the last king to be born in Scotland.
1645	The last major smallpox epidemic in Scotland.

1688   The last of the Stewart monarchs, James VII (and II of England) fled to France.

1695   The first bank in Scotland, the Bank of Scotland, was founded.

1725   The first circulating library in Great Britain was started by Allan Ramsay, the bookseller and poet from Leadhills.

1726   The first medical school in Scotland was established at Edinburgh University.

1728   The Royal Bank of Scotland introduced the overdraft system.

1736   The first public theatre in Scotland was opened in Carruber's Close in Edinburgh.

1760   Thomas Braidwood (1715–1806) opened the first school for the deaf and dumb in Great Britain, in Edinburgh.

1768   The first Encyclopedia Brittanica was printed by William Smellie.

1777   The first coloured banknote in Scotland produced by the Royal Bank of Scotland (one guinea, soon withdrawn).

1784   James 'Balloon' Tytler made the first ascent in a hot air balloon in Scotland.

1801   The first national census was made in Scotland.

1807   The first museum in Scotland, The Hunterian Museum, was founded.

1813   The last great auk in Great Britain was killed on Papa Westray, Orkney.

1824   The first municipal fire brigade in the world was founded in Edinburgh, under the leadership of James Braidwood.

1831   The first passenger rail service in Scotland opened on the line between Glasgow and Garnkirk.

1842   Queen Victoria and Prince Albert made their first visit to Scotland.

1847   The horse-drawn mail coach made its last journey from Edinburgh to London.

1850   The first railway ferry in the world came into use in Scotland, carrying goods wagons from Granton near Edinburgh to Burntisland in Fife.

1860   The first open golf championship was held in Scotland, at St Andrews.

1853   First use of chloroform at a royal birth, by James Young Simpson, at the birth of Prince Leopold to Queen Victoria.

1862   The last woman to be publicly executed in Scotland, Mary Anne Timney, was executed at Dumfries for the murder of a neighbour.

1868   The last public hanging in Scotland took place in Dumfries. Robert Smith was executed for murder.

1871   The first municipally funded museum in Scotland opened in Paisley.

1878   The first governing body for state-run prisons, the Scottish Prison Commission, came into being.

1888   The first convict prison in Scotland was opened at Peterhead. The term 'convicts' applied at that time to prisoners who had been sentenced to penal servitude. Until Peterhead came into being, prisoners sentenced to hard labour were sent to England.

1894   Marion Gilchrist (1864–1952) became the first woman to graduate from Glasgow University and the first woman to graduate in medicine in Scotland.

1899   The Clydesdale Bank became the first bank in Scotland to use adding machines.

1915   The first outpatient antenatal clinic in Britain was opened at the Edinburgh Royal Maternity and Simpson Memorial Maternity Pavilion, Edinburgh.

1923   The first radio broadcasts in Scotland were made in Rex House, Bath Street, Glasgow.

1923   On 10th October, 1923, Susan Newell was hanged in Duke Street Prison, Glasgow for the murder of a boy. She was the last woman to be executed in Scotland.

1930   On August 21, Princess Margaret Rose was born, the first royal baby to be born in Scotland since Charles I (1600).

1930   On August 29, the last inhabitants left St Kilda

1939   The first enemy air raids of World War II on Scotland were made on the Forth Estuary.

1945   On the 7th May, the last enemy attack of World War II on British territory took place in the Forth Estuary. Two allied ships (*Avondale Park*, a British ship and *Sneland I*, a Norwegian vessel) were sunk by U-boat torpedoes.

1946   The first settlement of Cistercian monks in Scotland since the Reformation was founded at Nunraw, Haddington, East Lothian.

1947   The first Edinburgh Festival was launched

1948   The first mobile bank branches were introduced by the Clydesdale Bank.

1952   The first television broadcasts went out in Scotland.
The first television play made in Scotland was by J M Barrie – 'The Old Lady Shows her Medals'.
The first outside broadcast made in Scotland was of the Edinburgh Military Tattoo.

1958   The Clydesdale Bank became the first Scottish bank to introduce personal loans.

1959   The first nuclear power station in Scotland was opened at Chapelcross in Dumfriesshire.

1960   The first moving picture of Nessie, the Loch Ness Monster, was taken.

1963   The last hanging in Scotland was carried out at Craiginches prison, Aberdeen, on August 15. Henry John Burnett was hanged for the murder of a seaman.

1966   The Clydesdale Bank became the first bank in Britain to supply customers with cheque guarantee cards.

1966   Sir James Arnot Hamilton, a Scot, became the first director-general of the Concorde project.

1966   Glasgow Celtic became the first British side to win the European Cup, beating Inter Milan 2–1 in Lisbon.

1975   The first North Sea oil was piped to the Scottish mainland at Peterhead.

1976   John Ogilvie of Keith was canonised, becoming the first Scottish saint since St Margaret (canonised 1250).

1977   The first successful cloning of an animal in the world was achieved with the birth of Dolly the Sheep at the Roslin Institute in Edinburgh.

1978   Grace MacDonald from Denny became the first Scottish woman – and the second in the world – to give birth to a 'test-tube' baby. The baby was a boy, named Alastair.

1997   Mohammed Sarwar was elected as the first Muslim MP in Scotland, serving the constituency of Govan, Glasgow (Labour).

1999   On May 12, the 129 members of the new devolved Scottish Parliament took their seats for the first time.

2001   Chef Gordon Ramsay is the first Scot to achieve three Michelin stars for a restaurant.

2003   In May, the last travelling post office (rail) operating from Scotland made its final journey from Glasgow to Cardiff.

2003   In July, Cameron Stout from Orkney became the first Scot to win the TV reality game show 'Big Brother'.

2006   Economist Adam Smith is the first Scot to appear on an English banknote

2007   The Scottish parliament has its first SNP government and First Minister, Alex Salmond. This is also its first minority government. SNP Bashir Ahmad becomes the first Asian MSP.

2008   In Beijing, Scottish track cyclist Chris Hoy becomes the first British Olympian to win three gold medals in one games since 1908.

SCOTTISH CATTLE BREEDS

Aberdeen Angus
Ayrshire
Galloway (Including White and
Belted Galloway)
Highland
Luing
Shetland

SCOTTISH HORSE BREEDS

Clydesdale Horse
Eriskay Pony
Highland Pony
Shetland Pony

SCOTTISH SHEEP BREEDS

Blackface (also known as Scottish Blackface, Blackfaced Highland, Scottish
Highland, Scottish Mountain, Scotch Horn)
Boreray (also known as Boreray Blackface)
Castlemilk Moorit
Hebridean (also known as St Kilda)
North Country Cheviot
North Ronaldsay (also known as Orkney)
Shetland
Soay
South Country Cheviot

FORMER OCCUPATIONS OF FAMOUS SCOTS

Robert Burns, poet and songwriter ....Farmer, exciseman
Thomas Carlyle, historian ....Teacher
Andrew Carnegie, industrialist...Railway clerk
William Collins, publisher...Weaver
Sean Connery, international film star.. Milkman
Billy Connolly, comedian and film and television actor...................... Welder
Sir Arthur Conan Doyle, author of 'Sherlock Holmes' mysteries ....Doctor
Sir Alexander Fleming, bacteriologist...................................... Shipping clerk
Rikki Fulton, stage, film and television actor and comedian ..... Naval service
John Hannah, film and television actor... Electrician
Keir Hardie, founder of the Labour Party...........................Miner, journalist
James Kelman, novelist and Booker Prize winner .... Printer's apprentice
John Knox, leader of the Scottish Reformation ....Roman Catholic priest
Liz Lochhead, poet and dramatist.. Art teacher
James Maxton, 'Red Clydesider'..Teacher

William McGonagall, Scotland's worst poet.. Weaver

Bill Paterson, film and television actor .... Quantity surveyor

Sir Walter Scott, poet and novelist .... Advocate

Alastair Sim, stage and film actor.. Elocution lecturer

Bill Simpson, actor (Dr Finlay's Casebook):........................... Insurance clerk

Mary Slessor, missionary... Mill worker

Dame Muriel Spark, novelist....................................Foreign Office employee

Sharleen Spiteri, lead singer, 'Texas'...Hairdresser

Robert Louis Stevenson, writer.. Advocate

Thomas Telford, civil engineer..Stonemason

Richard Wilson, stage, film and television actor................. Research scientist

CITY TRANSPORT IN SCOTLAND

1871	First horse-drawn tram in Edinburgh
1872	First horse-drawn tram in Glasgow
1874	First horse-drawn tram in Aberdeen
1877	First horse-drawn tram in Dundee
1885	Steam trams introduced in Dundee
1896	First (and only) underground railway in Scotland opened in Glasgow
1898	Cable car system introduced in Edinburgh
1898	First motor bus in Edinburgh
1898	First electric tram in Edinburgh
1898	First electric tram in Glasgow
1899	First electric tram line opens in Aberdeen
1900	First electric trams running in Dundee
1920	First Corporation bus in Aberdeen
1922	Cable cars replaced by electric trams in Edinburgh
1928	First motor bus running in Dundee
1902	Last steam tramcar in Dundee
1902	Last horse-drawn tram in Glasgow
1907	Last horse-drawn tram in Edinburgh
1908	First trolleybus in Dundee
1920	First motor bus running in Glasgow
1949	First trolleybus running in Glasgow
1954	Last electric tram journey in Aberdeen
1956	Last electric tram journey in Edinburgh (trams to return in 2011)
1956	Last electric tram journey in Dundee
1962	Last electric tram journey in Glasgow
1967	Last trolleybus journey in Glasgow

RUGBY MISCELLANY

1871   First Scotland v England international, held at Raeburn Place, Edinburgh. Scotland won!

1873   Founding of the Scottish Football Union, later to become the Scottish Rugby Union

1883   First rugby sevens game, played at Melrose

1905   First rugby international against New Zealand. Scotland lost 12–7

•   Highest points scorer for Scotland in rugby internationals: Chris Paterson (693)

•   Most capped player for Scotland: Chris Paterson

SCOTTISH VICTORIES IN THE FOUR/FIVE/SIX NATIONS CHAMPIONSHIP

1886 ....(shared with England)

1887

1890 ....(shared with England)

1891

1895

1901

1903

1904

1907

1920 (shared with England and Wales)

1925 ....GRAND SLAM!

1926 ....(shared with Ireland)

1927 ....(shared with Ireland)

1929

1933

1938

1964 ....(shared with Wales)

1973 ....(shared with England, ...Ireland, Wales and France)

1984 ....GRAND SLAM!

1986 ....(shared with France)

1990 ....GRAND SLAM!

1999

SCOTLAND v ENGLAND RUGBY MATCHES: WINNERS 1871–2004

1871	Scotland	1879	Draw
1872	England	1880	England
1873	England	1881	Draw
1874	England	1882	Scotland
1875	Draw	1883	England
1876	England	1884	England
1877	Scotland	1885	no match
1878	Draw	1886	Draw

1887	Draw	1931	Scotland
1888	no match	1932	England
1889	no match	1933	Scotland
1890	England	1934	England
1891	Scotland	1935	Scotland
1892	England	1936	England
1893	Scotland	1937	England
1894	Scotland	1938	Scotland
1895	Scotland	1939–46	no matches
1896	Scotland	1947	England
1897	England	1948	Scotland
1898	Draw	1949	England
1899	Scotland	1950	Scotland
1900	Draw	1951	England
1901	Scotland	1952	England
1902	England	1953	England
1903	Scotland	1954	England
1904	Scotland	1955	England
1905	Scotland	1956	England
1906	Scotland	1957	England
1907	Scotland	1958	Draw
1908	Scotland	1959	Draw
1909	Scotland	1960	England
1910	England	1961	England
1911	England	1962	Draw
1912	England	1963	England
1913	England	1964	Scotland
1914–19	no matches	1965	Draw
1920	England	1966	Scotland
1921	England	1967	England
1922	England	1968	England
1923	England	1969	England
1924	England	1970	Scotland
1925	Scotland	1971	Scotland
1926	Scotland	1972	Scotland
1927	Scotland	1973	England
1928	England	1974	Scotland
1929	Scotland	1975	England
1930	Draw	1976	Scotland

1977	England	1993	England
1978	England	1994	England
1979	Draw	1995	England
1980	England	1996	England
1981	England	1997	England
1982	Draw	1998	England
1983	Scotland	1999	England
1984	Scotland	2000	Scotland
1985	England	2001	England
1986	Scotland	2002	England
1987	England	2003	England
1988	England	2004	England
1989	England	2005	England
1990	Scotland	2006	Scotland
1991	England	2007	England
1992	England	2008	Scotland

BORDERERS
Did you know ... ?

Berwick Rangers FC are the only English football team to play in the Scottish league. Likewise, the club is the only Scottish league team to play its home fixtures on English ground.

FOOTBALL MISCELLANY

The Scots are passionate about football, and although their national team has not managed to secure any major successes in recent years, several Scottish clubs have established themselves as important players on the European scene.

- The record for the most number of goals scored for Scotland (30), is shared between Denis Law and Kenny Dalglish.
- When he first stepped onto the pitch for his country, aged eighteen, Dennis Law was the youngest player to be capped for Scotland.
- The first floodlit football match in Scotland was played at Ibrox (Rangers v Queen of the South) in March 1956.

- Jimmy McGrory (1904–1982), who played for Celtic, scored a record total of 410 goals in 408 league matches during his career.
- The record for the biggest ever football crowd in Europe is held by Hampden. In 1937, 149, 547 spectators attended a match between Scotland and England at the ground.

INTERESTING FOOTBALL CLUB NICKNAMES

Almost every football club in Scotland, from Sunday league to Premier League, has a nickname. Many of them are obvious – 'The Saints', 'The Rovers' etc. This is a list of some of the more interesting and less obvious nicknames.

Airdrie United	The Diamonds
Arbroath FC	The Red Lichties
Ayr United FC	The Honest Men
Clyde FC	The Bully Wee
Cowdenbeath FC	The Blue Brazil
Deveronvale FC	The Valley Crew
Dumbarton FC	The Sons
Dundee United FC	The Terrors, The Arabs, Tangerines
Dunfermline Athletic FC	The Pars
Falkirk FC	The Bairns
Forfar Athletic FC	The Loons
Glasgow Celtic FC	The Bhoys
Glasgow Celtic (European Cup team, 1967)	The Lisbon Lions
Glasgow Rangers FC	The Teddy Bears/ Gers
Livingston FC (formerly Meadowbank Thistle)	The Livvy Lions
Montrose FC	The Gable Endies
Motherwell FC	The Steelmen, The Dossers, The Well
Partick Thistle FC	The Jags
Peterhead FC	The Bloo Toon
Queen of the South FC	The Doonhammers
Queen's Park FC	The Spiders
St Mirren FC	The Buddies
Stenhousemuir FC	The Warriors
Stirling Albion FC	The Binos
Third Lanark FC (no longer in existence)	The Hi-His

SCOTTISH CUP WINNERS 1873–2008

1873 ....Queen's Park	1910 .... Dundee
1874 ....Queen's Park	1911 ....Celtic
1875 ....Queen's Park	1912 ....Celtic
1876 ....Queen's Park	1913 ....Falkirk
1877 ....Vale of Leven	1914 ....Celtic
1878 ....Vale of Leven	1915–1919 .... no matches
1879 ....Vale of Leven	1920 ....Kilmarnock
1880 ....Queen's park	1921 ....Partick Thistle
1881 ....Queen's Park	1922 ....Morton
1882 ....Queen's Park	1923 ....Celtic
1883 .... Dumbarton	1924 ....Airdrie
1884 ....Queen's Park	1925 ....Celtic
1885 .... Renton	1926 ....St Mirren
1886 ....Queen's Park	1927 ....Celtic
1887 ....Hibernian	1928 .... Rangers
1888 .... Renton	1929 ....Kilmarnock
1889 ....Third Lanark	1930 .... Rangers
1890 ....Queen's Park	1931 ....Celtic
1891 ....Heart of Midlothian	1932 .... Rangers
1892 ....Celtic	1933 ....Celtic
1893 ....Queen's Park	1934 .... Rangers
1894 .... Rangers	1935 .... Rangers
1895 ....St Bernard's	1936 .... Rangers
1896 ....Heart of Midlothian	1937 ....Celtic
1897 .... Rangers	1938 .... East Fife
1898 .... Rangers	1939 ....Clyde
1899 ....Celtic	1940–46 .... no matches
1900 ....Celtic	1947 ....Aberdeen
1901 ....Heart of Midlothian	1948 .... Rangers
1902 ....Hibernian	1949 .... Rangers
1903 .... Rangers	1950 .... Rangers
1904 ....Celtic	1951 ....Celtic
1905 ....Third Lanark	1952 ....Motherwell
1906 ....Heart of Midlothian	1953 .... Rangers
1907 ....Celtic	1954 ....Celtic
1908 ....Celtic	1955 .... Clyde
1909 .... cup withheld	1956 ....Hearts

1957 .... Falkirk	1983 .... Aberdeen
1958 .... Clyde	1984 .... Aberdeen
1959 .... St Mirren	1985 .... Celtic
1960 ....Rangers	1986 .... Aberdeen
1961 ....Dunfermline	1987 .... St Mirren
1962 ....Rangers	1988 .... Celtic
1963 ....Rangers	1989 .... Celtic
1964 ....Rangers	1990 .... Aberdeen
1965 .... Celtic	1991 .... Motherwell
1966 ....Rangers	1992 ....Rangers
1967 .... Celtic	1993 ....Rangers
1968 ....Dunfermline	1994 ....Dundee United
1969 .... Celtic	1995 .... Celtic
1970 .... Aberdeen	1996 ....Rangers
1971 .... Celtic	1997 ....Kilmarnock
1971 .... Celtic	1998 ....Heart of Midlothian
1973 ....Rangers	1999 ....Rangers
1974 .... Celtic	2000 ....Rangers
1975 .... Celtic	2001 .... Celtic
1976 ....Rangers	2002 ....Rangers
1977 .... Celtic	2003 ....Rangers
1978 ....Rangers	2004 .... Celtic
1979 ....Rangers	2005 .... Celtic
1980 .... Celtic	2006 ....Heart of Midlothian
1981 ....Rangers	2007 .... Celtic
1982 .... Aberdeen	2008 ....Rangers

THE LAST WOLF IN SCOTLAND
Did you know ... ?

There are four possible places where the last wolf is said to have been killed in Scotland (there may be others!) 1680, near Killiecrankie, by Ewan Cameron of Lochiel. Brora, Sutherland, around 1700. Perpetrator unknown. 1743, Perthshire, by Ewan MacQueen. 1743, Morayshire – a killing allegedly carried out by people of the district in revenge for the deaths of two children.

THE DAYS OF THE WEEK IN GAELIC

Sunday: Di-dòmhnaich
Monday: Di-luain
Tuesday: Di-màirt
Wednesday: Di-ceudain
Thursday: Dior-daoin
Friday: Di-h-aoine
Saturday: Di-Sathuirne

THE MONTHS OF THE YEAR IN GAELIC

January: Am Faolteach
February: An Gearran
March: Am Màrt
April: An Giblin
May: An Céitean
June: An t-Og-mhios
July: An t-Iuchar
August: An Lùnasdal
September: An t-Sultùine
October: An Dàmhar
November: An t-Samhainn
December: An Dùdlachd

SCOTTISH REGIMENTS AND BATALLIONS

The Royal Regiment of Scotland

In 2006, as part of restructuring the British Army, five regular and two territorial Scottish infantry battalions (previously regiments) were merged into a single large regiment, the Royal Regiment of Scotland. This move was highly emotive and controversial. It also involved the amalgamation of the Royal Scots and The King's Own Scottish Borderers to form the Royal Scots Borderers.

Regimental Headquarters: Edinburgh Castle
Tartan: Government (otherwise known as The Black Watch tartan)
Colonel-in-Chief: HM Queen Elizabeth II
Motto: *Nemo Nos Impune Lacessit* (No-one assails us with impunity)

The Royal Scots Borderers (Light Role)
The King's Own Scottish Borderers was raised in 1689. The Royal Scots regiment was raised in 1633. In 2006, the regiments merged to become the Royal Scots Borderers, 1st Battalion of the The Royal Regiment of Scotland.
Headquarters: Dreghorn Barracks, Edinburgh.
Tartan: Government, Royal Stewart
Royal Colonel: HRH Princess Anne, The Princess Royal
Motto: *Nemo me impune lacessit* (No-one assails me with impunity).

The Royal Highland Fusiliers (Light Role)
In 1959, The Royal Scots Fusiliers (raised in 1678) and The Highland Light Infantry (71st, raised in 1777 and 74th, raised in 1787) were amalgamated to form the Royal Highland Fusiliers. In 2006 the regiment was amalgamated with the other regiments of the Scottish Division to become The Royal Highland Fusiliers, 2nd batallion, the Royal Regiment of Scotland.
Headquarters: Glencorse Barracks, Penicuik
Tartan: Government, Red Erskine
Royal Colonel: HRH Prince Andrew, The Duke of York
Motto: *Nemo me Impune Lacessit* (No-one assails me with impunity).

The Black Watch (Light Role)
Raised as six independent companies in 1725. Formed, with the addition of four more companies, into a regiment in 1739. In 2006 the regiment was amalgamated with the other regiments of the Scottish Division to become The Black Watch, 3rd Battalion, Royal Regiment of Scotland.
Regimental Headquarters: Fort George
Tartans: The Black Watch (Government), Royal Stewart
Royal Colonel: HRH Prince Charles, Duke of Rothesay
Motto: *Nemo me Impune Lacessit* (No-one assails me with impunity).

The Highlanders (Armoured Infantry)
In 1994, the Queen's Own Highlanders and The Gordon Highlanders (75th, raised in 1787 and 92nd, raised in 1794) were amalgamated to form The Highlanders. The Queen's Own Highlanders had been formed in 1961 from an amalgamation of The Seaforth Highlanders (72nd, raised in 1778 and 78th, raised in 1793) and The Queen's Own Cameron Highlanders (raised in 1793). In 2006 the regiment was amalgamated with the other regiments of the

Scottish Division to become The Highlanders 4th Battalion, Royal Regiment of Scotland.

Headquarters: Fallingbostel, Germany
Tartans: Government, Cameron of Erracht
Royal Colonel: HRH The Prince Philip, Duke of Edinburgh
Motto: *Nemo me Impune Lacessit* (No-one assails me with impunity)

The Argyll and Sutherland Highlanders (Air Assault)
Formed from The 91st Scottish Highland Infantry (raised in 1794) and The 93rd Scottish Highland Infantry (raised in 1799). In 2006 the regiment was amalgamated with the other regiments of the Scottish Division to become The Argyll and Sutherland Highlanders 5th Battalion, Royal Regiment of Scotland.

Headquarters: Canterbury
Tartan: Government, Sutherland
Royal Colonel: HM Queen Elizabeth II
Mottoes: *Nemo me Impune Lacessit* (No-one assails me with impunity).

52nd Lowland (TA Reserve, Light Role)
The 6th Battalion of the Royal Regiment of Scotland
Headquarters: Glasgow
Tartan: Government, Red Erskine
Royal Colonel: HRH Princess Anne, The Princess Royal
Motto: *Nemo me Impune Lacessit* (No-one assails me with impunity).

51st Highland (TA Reserve, Light Role)
The 7th Battalion of the Royal Regiment of Scotland
Headquarters: Perth
Tartan: Government
Royal Colonel: HRH Prince Charles, Duke of Rothesay
Motto: *Nemo me Impune Lacessit* (No-one assails me with impunity).

The Royal Scots Dragoon Guards (Carabiniers and Greys)

In 1971, The Royal Scots Greys (Second Dragoons) and The 3rd Carabiniers (Prince of Wales's Dragoon Guards) were amalgamated to form The Royal Scots Dragoon Guards.

Regimental Headquarters: Edinburgh Castle
Colonel-in-Chief: HM Queen Elizabeth II
Motto: *Nemo me Impune Lacessit* (No-one assails me with impunity).

The Scots Guards (Infantry)

Raised in 1642.

Regimental Headquarters: Birdcage Walk, London

Tartan: Royal Stewart

Colonel-in-Chief: HM Queen Elizabeth II

Motto: *Nemo Me Impune Lacessit* (No-one assails me with impunity).

SCOTTISH PIONEERS
Did you know ... ?

I n Sydney Park, Australia, there stands a cairn with a stone from every parish in Scotland. It was erected as a memorial to all the Scottish Pioneers who played such an important role in shaping the country.

CLAN BADGES, CRESTS AND MOTTOES

In centuries past, when clan members were called upon to fight for their chief, they would commonly wear a sprig from a plant or a tree associated with their clan, in order to identify themselves in battle. The clan crest is a heraldic device, officially recognised by the Lord Lyon King of Arms. It is the property of the chief and he alone has the right to wear it. The custom of wearing badges as ornament to demonstrate membership of a particular clan is relatively recent. These badges consist of silver brooches, showing the crest of the chief encircled by a belt, which symbolises clansmanship.

	Clan Bruce
Plant Badge	Rosemary
Clan Motto	*Fuimus* (We Have Been)
Clan Crest	A lion

	Clan Campbell
Plant Badges	Bog myrtle, fir club moss
Clan Motto	*Ne Obliviscaris* (Forget Not).
	Campbells of Breadalbane: Follow Me.
	Campbells of Loudon: I Bide My Time.

Campbells of Cawdor: Be Mindful.

Clan Crest   Boar's Head.

Campbells of Loudon: Double-headed eagle.

Campbells of Cawdor: Crowned Swan

Clan Cameron

Plant Badges   Oak, crowberry

Clan Motto   *Aonaibh Re Cheile* (Unite)

Clan Crest   Sheaf of five arrows

Clan Crawford

Plant Badge   Boxwood

Clan Motto   *Tutum Robore Reddam* (I Will Make You Safe With Strength)

Clan Crest   A stag's head with a cross between the antlers

Clan Davidson

Plant Badge   Red whortleberry

Clan Motto   *Sapienter Si Sincere* (Wisely if Sincerely)

Clan Crest   Stag's head

Clan Douglas

Clan Motto   *Jamais Arriere* (Never Behind)

Clan Crest   A salamander encircled by flames

Clan Erskine

Clan Motto   *Je Pense Plus* (I Think More)

Clan Crest   A right hand holding a dagger

Clan Fraser

Plant Badges   Yew, strawberry

Clan Motto   All My Hope Is In God.

Clan Crest   Flourish of strawberries

Clan Farquharson

Plant Badge   Scots fir

Clan Motto   *Fide et Fortitudine* (With Fidelity and Strength)

Can Crest   Half lion, holding a sword

Clan Forbes

Plant Badge	Broom
Clan Motto	Grace Me Guide
Clan Crest	A stag's head

Clan Gordon

Plant Badge	Rock Ivy
Clan Mottoes	Bydand (Abiding), Do well and let them say – Gordon
Clan Crest	A buck's head above a coronet

Clan Graham

Plant Badge	Laurel
Clan Motto	*Ne Oublie* (Do Not Forget)
Clan Crest	Falcon, wings outstretched, attacking a stork

Clan Grant

Plant Badge	Pine
Clan Motto	Stand Fast
Clan Crest	The rock of Craigellachie encircled by flames

Clan Gregor

Plant Badge	Scots fir
Clan Motto	*Is Rioghal Mo Dhream* (Royal Is My Race)
Clan Crest	A lion's head with a coronet

Clan Hamilton

Plant Badge	Rock Ivy
Clan Motto	*Animo Non Astutia* (By Courage Not Craft)
Clan Crest	An oak above a coronet, with a frame cutting through the tree

Clan Keith

Plant Badge	White rose
Clan Motto	*Veritas vinci* (Truth Conquers)
Clan Crest	A roe buck's head emerging from a gold coronet

Clan Kennedy

Plant Badge	Oak
Clan Motto	*Avise la Fin* (Consider the End)
Clan Crest	A dolphin

Clan Lindsay

Plant Badges	Rue, lime tree
Clan Motto	*Endure Fort* (Endure with Strength)
Clan Crest	Head, neck and wings of swan, emerging from coronet

Clan Kerr

Plant Badge	Moss myrtle
Clan Motto	*Sero Sed Serio* (Late But In Earnest)
Clan Crest	The sun in splendour

Clan Macdonald

Plant Badges	Heather, ling
Clan Motto	*Per Mare Per Terras* (By Sea and By Land)
Clan Crest	An armoured hand holding a cross

Clan MacDougall

Plant Badge	Bell heather
Clan Motto	*Buaidh no Bas* (Conquer or Die)
Clan Crest	A right arm in armour holding a cross

Clan MacDuff

Plant Badges	Red whortleberry, holly
Clan Motto	*Deus Juvat* (God Assists)
Clan Crest	A lion rampant, holding a dagger in its right paw

Clan Mackay

Plant Badge	Great bulrush
Clan Motto	*Manu Forti* (With a Strong Hand)
Clan Crest	A dagger held by a right hand

Clan MacKenzie

Plant Badge	Holly
Clan Motto	*Luceo Non Uro* (I Shine Not Burn)
Clan Crest	Stag's head

Clan Mackintosh

Plant Badges	Red whortleberry, cranberry
Clan Motto	Touch Not the Cat Bot a Glove
Clan Crest	Wild cat (rampant)

Clan MacLean

Plant Badges	Crowberry, holly
Clan Motto	Virtue Mine Honour
Clan Crest	Tower with battlements

Clan MacLeod

Plant Badges	Juniper, Whortleberry
Clan Mottoes	MacLeod of MacLeod: Hold Fast.
	MacLeod of Lewis: I Burn While I See
Clan Crest	Bull's head between two flags

Clan Macmillan

Plant Badge	Holly
Clan Motto	*Miseris Succere Disco* (I Learn to Succour the Unfortunate)
Clan Crest	Two hands holding a claymore

Clan MacNeil

Plant Badges	Dryas, mountain avens
Clan Motto	*Vincere Vel Mor* (Conquer or Die)
Clan Crest	A rock

Clan Macpherson

Plant Badge	Variegated boxwood, white heather
Clan Motto	Touch Not the Cat Without a Glove
Clan Crest	Seated wild cat

Clan MacRae

Plant Badges	Stag's horn moss, fir club moss
Clan Motto	*Fortitudine* (With Strength)
Clan Crest	A hand holding a sword

Clan Menzies

Plant Badges	Menzies heath, rowan
Clan Motto	*Vil God I Zal* (With God I Shall)
Clan Crest	A savage head

Clan Morrison

Plant Badge	Driftwood
Clan Motto	Teaglach Phabbay (Family of Pabbay)
Clan Crest	A turreted castle rising from the waves, with a hand holding a dagger emerging from it

Clan Murray

Plant badges	Butcher's broom, juniper
Clan Motto	Furth Fortune and Fill the Fetters
Clan Crest	A demi-savage holding a dagger in his right hand, a key in his left

Clan Ogilvie

Plant Badge	Hawthorn
Clan Motto	*A Fin* (To the End)
Clan Crest	Naked woman, holding a portcullis

Clan Roberston

Plant Badge	Bracken
Clan Motto	*Virtutis Gloria Merces* (Glory Is the Reward of Valour)
Clan Crest	A right hand holding a crown

Clan Ross

Plant Badge	Juniper
Clan Motto	*Spem Successus Alit* (Success Nourishes Hope)
Clan Crest	A hand holding a laurel wreath

Clan Scott

Plant Badge	Blaeberry
Clan Motto	*Je Suis Prest* (I Am Ready)
Clan Crest	A stag

Clan Sinclair

Plant Badge	White Clover
Clan Motto	Commit Thy Work to God
Clan Crest	Cockerel

Clan Stewart

Plant Badges   Thistle, oak

Clan Mottoes   Virescit Vulnere Virtus (Courage Grows Strong at the Wound).

Stewarts of Appin: Nobilis Est Ira Leonis (Noble Is the Wrath of the·Lion)

Stewarts of Balquhidder: *Quhidder Will Zie* (Whither Will Ye)

Clan Crest   A pelican feeding her young in the nest

Clan Wallace

Plant Badge   Oak

Clan Motto   Pro Libertate (For Freedom)

Clan Crest   Arm in armour, holding sword

THE LORD'S PRAYER IN SCOTS

Oor Faither wha bides in heiven,
Hallowt be thy name;
Thy Kinrick come;
Thy will be dune
In the yird, as in the lan o' the leal.
Gie us wir breid ilk day;
An forgie us wir ill-daein,
As oo forgie the yins wha wrang us;
An sey-us-na sairlie,
But sauf us frae provokshin.
For aye, thine's the Kinrick, the pooer, the glore
Amen

BURNS SUPPER

The life of Scotland's greatest poet has been celebrated in Scotland for more than two hundred years. It is thought that the first Burns Supper was held by friends of Robert Burns not long after he died, to recognise his birthday and pay tribute to his achievements. Burns Suppers can be either formal or casual affairs and can involve any number of people, from a small group of friends to a gathering of more than one hundred people. The basic format varies little – the pomp and ceremony with which it is carried through very much depends on the formality of the circumstances.

Date: January 25th

Suggested Menu

Cock-a-Leekie Soup/Cullen Skink
Haggis, Neeps and Champit Tatties
Cranachan/sherry trifle
(Choice of starter and dessert can vary, but haggis is essential)

Arriving guests should be offered a drink – whisky is traditional, but wine is acceptable. Once the party has assembled at table, the evening should proceed as follows:

1 Chairman's welcome.
2 Grace – The Selkirk Grace (see below)
3 After the first course has been cleared away the haggis is 'piped in' – i.e., carried to the table by the chef, who is accompanied by a piper playing a stirring tune.
4 The chairman, or another elected speaker, gives the Address to the Haggis. (see below). The address should be given with enthusiasm and the speaker should have a knife beside him, ready to plunge into the haggis at the appropriate moment in the poem:

> 'An' cut you up wi' ready slight
> Trenching your gushing entrails bright
> Like onie ditch.'

When the address is over, the guests toast the haggis with whisky.
5 After the address, the haggis, neeps and tatties are served to the guests.
6 When the meal is over, the chairman, or another elected speaker, makes the first speech – The Immortal Memory. The speech should pay tribute to aspects of the life and work of Robert Burns.
7 The Toast to the Lasses. This should be a light-hearted tribute to ladies present and may recall some of the many women in the bard's own life. It may be delivered in prose or rhyme. It should be humorous and may be teasing, but it should not be unkind.
8 The Lasses Response. An elected female member of the party takes the opportunity to make a witty reply to the Toast to the Lasses, either in prose or in rhyme.
9 With the formalities of the evening over, the rest of the night is generally spent enjoying the songs and poems of Burns, performed by volunteers from among the guests.

THE SELKIRK GRACE

Although the Selkirk Grace is commonly attributed to Robert Burns, it is likely that it was in use before he wrote it down.

> Some hae meat and canna eat,
> And some wad eat that want it,
> But we hae meat and we can eat,
> And sae the Lord be thankit.

TO A HAGGIS

by Robert Burns

Fair fa' yer honest, sonsie face,
Great chieftain o' the Puddin-race!
Aboon them a' ye tak your place,
Painch, tripe, or thairm;
Weel are ye wordy of a grace
As lang's my arm.

The groaning trencher there ye fill,
Your hurdies like a distant hill,
Your pin wad help to mend a mill
In time o' need;
While thro' your pores the dews distil
Like amber bead.

His knife see rustic Labour dight,
An' cut you up wi' ready slight,
Trenching your gushing entrails bright
Like onie ditch;
And then, O what a glorious sight,
Warm-reekin', rich!

Then, horn for horn, they stretch an' strive,
Deil tak the hindmost, on they drive,
Till a' their weel-swall'd kytes belyve
Are bent like drums;
Then auld Guidman, maist like to rive,
'Bethankit' hums.

Is there that owre his French ragout
Or olio that wad staw a sow,
Or fricasee wad mak her spew
Wi' perfect sconner,
Looks down wi' sneering, scornfu' view
On sic a dinner?

Poor devil! See him owre his trash,,
As feckless as a wither'd rash,
His spindle shank a guid whip-lash,
His nieve a nit;
Thro' bluidy flood or field to dash,
O how unfit!

But mark the Rustic, haggis-fed,
The trembling earth resounds his tread,
Clap in his walie nieve a blade,
He'll mak it whissle;
An' legs an' arms an' heads will sned
Like taps o' thrissle.

Ye Pow'rs wha mak mankind your care,
And dish them out their bill o' fare,
Auld Scotland wants nae skinking ware,
That jaups in luggies;
But, if ye wish yer gratefu' prayer,
Gie her a Haggis!

THE BITING MIDGE: SCOURGE
OF THE SCOTTISH HIGHLANDS

- Gaelic name: *meanbh-chuileag*
- Species: *Culicoides Impunctatus*
- Family: Chironomidae
- Order: Diptera
- Favoured breeding ground: boggy, acidic soil provides the optimum conditions for larvae to develop.
- Development: If eggs are laid early, in a mild spring, the adult midges may emerge before summer is past. When fertilisation takes place in summer,

the larva take longer to develop, overwintering in the soil before emerging as adults from May to July.

- Average lifespan of an adult midge: 20–30 days
- Most active biting period: July to August
- Likes: Grey skies, low light levels, windless conditions. Breeding females only – mammal blood.
- Dislikes: Bright sunshine, breezy conditions.
- Attracted by: Dark colours, moving objects, carbon dioxide (given off in human breath) and other chemicals in mammal body odour.

Frequently Asked Questions About Midges

Q: Do all midges bite?

A: No. *Culicoides Impunctatus* is only one of approximately 1,500 species of midge found all over the world, most of which are non-biting.

Q: Why do they bite?

A: Contrary to popular belief, *Culicoides Impunctatus* is not a vindictive creature. The breeding females of this species bite because they need to feed on blood after mating, so that their eggs can develop successfully.

Q: Do they only bite humans?

A: No. They feed on other mammals too – in particular, the Scottish midge sucks the blood from deer, cattle and sheep.

Q: Are they only found in Scotland?

A: No. Biting midges can be found in other European countries, but they do seem to find Scotland, and in particular, the north and west of the country, particularly suitable for their lifestyle.

Q: How much blood do they take?

A: Very little – they are tiny creatures. But as long as they are left undisturbed, they will suck until they are full to bursting. This can take more than three minutes. If one midge is biting you, it is likely that several will. When a midge finds a victim, it gives off a chemical signal to inform all others in the vicinity that dinner is served.

Q: How can I avoid them?

A: Stay away from areas of damp, low ground during midge season (May to September), particularly on dull, windless or humid days in the months of July and August. Higher ground and coastal areas are safer, as there is more likely to be a stiff breeze to keep the little blighters at bay. Covering up offers some protection, but midges can still find their way up sleeves and trouser legs, down collars, etc. Use insect repellent liberally, but don't expect miracles.

GAELIC PRONUNCIATION: A VERY BASIC GUIDE

There are eighteen letters in the Gaelic alphabet: A, B, C, D, E, F, G, H, I, L, M, N, O, P, R, S, T, U.

The thirteen consonants, in most circumstances, are pronounced in the same way as in the English language, but their pronunciation may alter according to their position in a word. For example 'b' is pronounced like the English 'b' at the beginning of a word, but in the middle of a word, it is pronounced like 'p'. The sounds of consonants can also be modified when they are combined with other consonants or vowels. For example, when combined with the aspirate 'h', the sounds of the letters c, d, f, g, m, p, s and t change significantly. And when 's' is followed by 'i' or 'e', its sound changes to 'sh'.

The vowel sounds in Gaelic may be either short (unaccented) or long.

Consonant Sounds

b: Hard, as in the English words 'bet', or 'bag', or softer, as in 'soapy'.

bh: In most cases, pronounced like 'v'. It is pronounced as 'u' in the middle or at the end of some words. Sometimes it is silent.

c: Pronounced hard, as in 'cat'.

ch: Generally pronounced as a gutteral sound, as in 'loch'.

chd: Pronounced as 'chk', with a gutteral 'ch'.

f: Pronounced the same as 'f' in English.

fh: In most cases, silent. Pronounced as 'h' in three words: *fhéin, fhuair, fhathast*.

g: Pronounced much like 'g' in English.

gh: If placed before 'i' or 'e', it sounds like 'y'. It can also be pronounced like 'gh' as in 'ugh'. Sometimes it is silent.

h: Breathy 'h' as in 'head', when positioned at the beginning of a word.

l :   longer and flatter than English 'l' sound – as in 'silly'.

ll: Pronounced like 'lli' in 'pillion'

m: Pronounced the same as 'm' in English.

mh: Pronounced like 'v', but is sometimes silent in the middle of a word. Sometimes it is pronounced as 'u'.

n: Similar to 'n' in English.

ng: Pronounced as 'ng' in 'finger', not 'singer'.

nn: Pronounced like 'ni' in 'opinion'.

p: Pronounced the same as an English 'p'.

ph: Pronounced as 'f'.

r: Pronounced with a distinct rolling sound.

S: Pronounced as 's' in English, unless it is placed before 'I' or 'e', when it becomes 'sh'.

Sh: Pronounced as 'h'.

T: Pronounced in a similar way to the English 't', but softer.

Th: Either silent, or pronounced as 'h'.

Basic Vowel Sounds

Short vowel sounds

a: as in 'c*a*t'

a: as in 'sof*a*'

e : as in 'b*e*t'

e: as in 'g*a*te'

i: as in 'm*i*lk'

Long vowel sounds

à: 'a' as in 'f*a*r'

è: as in 'where'

é: as in 'stair'

ì: as in 'tree'

ò: as in 'l*o*rd'

ó: as in 'm*o*re'

ù: 'oo' as in 'p*oo*l'

BONNIE PRINCE CHARLIE SLEPT HERE

Prince Charles Edward Stewart spent less than two years on British soil, but in that short time he moved around a great deal and slept in many different places. Forty places in Scotland where he is known, or believed, to have slept are listed below.

Balhadie House, Dunblane, Perthshire
Benbecula, Western Isles

Berneray, Outer Hebrides
Borrodale (The house of Angus Macdonald)
Braco, Perthshire (The Old House of Orchil)
Callander House, Falkirk
Castle Menzies, Perthshire
Castle Stuart, near Inverness
Cluny's Cage, Ben Alder (cave)
Culloden House (fortified house on the site of the
    present house), Inverness-shire
Dalnacardoch Lodge, Inverness-shire
Dalnaspidal Lodge, Glen Garry
Deans Mansion House, now known as Boghall
    House, Bathgate, West Lothian
Dimmindarich, near Mallaig (cave)
Drumlanrig Castle, Dumfries and Galloway
Drummond Arms Hotel, Crieff
Duddingston Village (Bonnie Prince Charlie's
    cottage), Edinburgh
Dunvegan Castle, Isle of Skye
Eriskay, Outer Hebrides
Fassfern House, Loch Eil
Glamis Castle, Tayside
Glen Affric, Beauly (Comar Lodge)
Gretna Green (Prince Charlie's Cottage)
Holyrood House, Edinburgh
Invergarry Castle, Glen Garry
Kelso (Chatto Lodging House, on the site now
    occupied by the Ednam House Hotel)
Kilravock Castle, near Inverness
King's Arms Hotel, Lockerbie
Kingsburgh House, Skye
Kinlochmoidart House, Kinlochmoidart
Linlithgow Palace
Mallaig (the house of Macdonald of Morar)
Moy Hall near Inverness
Pinkie House, Musselburgh
Portree, Isle of Skye (Bonnie Prince Charlie's
    cave, near Portree)
The Salutation hotel, Perth

Scalpay (Donald Campbell's House)
Thunderton House, near Elgin
Torvaig, Isle of Skye
Traquair House, near Peebles

NAME THAT PRINCE
Did you know... ?

HRH Prince Charles, the Prince of Wales has five Scottish titles:
Duke of Rothesay
Earl of Carrick
Baron Renfrew
Lord of the Isles
Great Steward of Scotland

MARY, QUEEN OF SCOTS SLEPT HERE

Mary, Queen of Scots travelled extensively around Scotland during the short period that she lived here. The following is a list of places where she is known or believed to have slept.

Balquhain Castle, Aberdeenshire
Balvenie Castle, Dufftown, Morayshire
Beauly Priory, near Inverness
Bishop's Palace, Clary, Wigtown
Blair Castle, Perthshire
Borthwick Castle, Midlothian
Cadzow Castle, Hamilton, Lanarkshire
Callendar House, Falkirk
Carrick Castle, Argyll
Cassiltoun Tower, Castlemilk
Castle Campbell, Dollar, Clackmannanshire
Craigmillar Castle, Edinburgh
Crookston Castle, Glasgow
Delgatie Castle, Turriff
Drumlanrig Castle, Nithsdale, Dumfriesshire

Drummond Castle, Perthshire
Dumbarton Castle, Dunbartonshire
Dunbar Castle, East Lothian
Dundrennan Abbey, Kirkcudbrightshire
Dunfermline Abbey
Dunnottar Castle, near Stonehaven
Dunoon Castle, Argyll
Dunure Castle, Ayrshire
Edinburgh Castle
Edzell Castle, Brechin, Angus
Falkland Palace, Fife
Gauldwell Castle, Morayshire
Glenluce Abbey, Dumfries and Galloway
Glamis Castle, Tayside
Hailes Castle, East Lothian
Hermitage Castle, Roxburghshire
Holyrood Palace, Edinburgh
Huntingtower Castle, Perthshire
Inchmahome Priory, Trossachs
Jedburgh (Mary Queen of Scots House)
Kilravock Castle, Inverness-shire
Kinloss Abbey, Morayshire
Leith (Andrew Lamb's House)
Linlithgow Palace
Lochleven Castle
Lochmaben Castle, Dumfriesshire
Loudon Hall, Ayr
Myres Castle, Auchtermuchty, Fife
Neidpath Castle, Peeblesshire
Niddry Castle, Winchburgh, West Lothian
Provand's Lordship, Glasgow
Rossend Castle, Burntisland
Spynie Palace, Elgin, Morayshire
St Andrews (Queen Mary's House, The Pends)
Stirling Castle
Strathendry Castle, Leslie, Fife
Traquair House, Innerleithen, Peeblesshire
Wedderburn Castle, Berwickshire
Wemyss Castle, Fife

TAGGART

Taggart is a detective drama series set in Glasgow, created in 1983 by Glenn Chandler, a pathologist turned writer, and Robert Love, the controller of drama at Scottish Television at the time. It still continues to be produced despite the death of its title character, the cantankerous and much-missed Jim Taggart, played unforgettably by Mark McManus. The first episode, 'Killer' (1983), was the only one without the *Taggart* series title. The series, in the format we now know, started in 1985. In excess of 90 episodes have been made by Scottish Television and it has been one of their most successful exports, sold all over the world and dubbed into several foreign languages.

Main Cast

Detective Chief Inspector Jim Taggart (1983–94) ....Mark McManus
Detective Sergeant/Detective Inspector/Detective Chief
    Inspector Mike Jardine (1987–2002) ....James McPherson
Detective Constable/Detective Sergeant Jackie Reid (1990–) ..... Blythe Duff
Detective Sergeant Peter Livingstone (1983–87) .... Neil Duncan
Superintendent Jack McVitie 'The Biscuit' (1985–98) .... Iain Anders
Dr Stephen Andrews, pathologist (1983–2001) .... Robert Robertson
Jean Taggart (1983–95) .... Harriet Buchan
Detective Constable Stuart Fraser (1995–) .... Colin McCredie
Detective Inspector Robbie Ross (1998–) ....John Michie
Detective Chief Inspector Matt Burke (2002–) ....Alex Norton
Superintendent Murray 'Murray Mint' (1983) ....Tom Watson
Alison Taggart (1983–95) .... Geraldine Alexander
Detective Superintendent Valerie Patterson (2002–)..........Anne Marie Timoney

Taggart Miscellany

- The show's writer Glenn Chandler is said to have found inspiration for the names of his characters, in the first episode, from graves in a Glasgow cemetery.
- *Taggart* is the longest running detective show on TV.
- Mike Jardine makes his first appearance as a minor character in 'The Killing Philosophy' (1986), and joins as major character in 'Funeral Rites' (1987).
- Before taking the role of Chief Inspector Matt Burke in 2002, Alex Norton previously appeared in *Taggart* as George Bryce in 'Knife Edge' (1986).
- John Michie also made a previous appearance before becoming DI Robbie Ross, as Robbie Meiklejohn in 'Love Knot' (1990).

- 'Black Orchid' (1995) was the first episode without Jim Taggart.
- Colin McCredie had minor roles, as Sandy in 'Hellfire' (1994), and in 'Prayer for the Dead' (1994) before becoming Stuart Fraser in 1995.
- 'Dead Reckoning' (1997) was the last episode with Ian Anders.
- In 'Few Bad Men' (1998) Jardine is promoted to DCI and Robbie Ross makes his first appearance.
- In 'Death Trap' (2002) Jardine is killed off and DCI Matt Burke joins the team.

Guest Stars

If often seems like the whole of the Scottish acting fraternity have at one time or another appeared in *Taggart*, sometimes more than once. Some of the guest stars who have appeared in *Taggart* are:

actor	character	episode
Louise Beattie	Karen Menzies	Puppet on a String (2005)
Maureen Beattie	Siobhan MacDonald	Ghost Rider (1999)
Maggie Bell	Euphemia Lambie	Evil Eye (1990)
Isla Blair	Lavinia Martin	Hellfire (1994)
Ewen Bremner	Jason	Love Knot (1990)
Juliet Cadzow	Maureen Macdonald	Nest of Vipers (1992)
Robert Carlyle	Gordon Inglis	Hostile Witness (1990)
Alan Cumming	Jamie McCormack	Death Call (1986)
Annette Crosbie	Maggie Davidson	Funeral Rites (1987)
Barbara Dickson	Marie McDonald	Legends (1995)
Alex Ferns	Lenny Kerr	Fearful Lightning (1999)
Jill Gascoigne	Jane Antrobus	Evil Eye (1990)
Hannah Gordon	Dr Janet Napier	Fatal Inheritance (1993)
Michelle Gomez	Harriet Bailes	Bloodlines (1998)
Clare P Grogan	Mary MacMurray	The Hitman (1992)
John Hannah	Danny Bonnar	Evil Eye (1990)
Douglas Henshall	motor cyclist	Love Knot (1990)
Diane Keen	Ruth Wilson	Cold Blood (1987)
Gerard Kelly	Graham Tully	Mind Over Matter (2005)
Simone Lahbib	Caroline Peterson	Nest of Vipers (1992)
	Sarah Stevenson	Prayer for the Dying (1994)
Phyllida Law	Joan Mathieson	Forbidden Fruit (1994)
John McGlynn	DCI McGarry	Evil Eye (1990)
Joseph McFadden	son of loan shark	Root of Evil (1988)
Francis Matthews	Dr Gerald Napier	Fatal Inheritance (1993)

Peter Mullen .... Peter Latimer....................Rogues' Gallery (1990)

.... Peter Lewis ....Love Knot (1990)

Peter O'Brien .... Bill Hamilton ....Death Without Dishonour (1993)

Amanda Redman .... Julie Carson........................ Black Orchid (1995)

Siobhan Redmond .... Judy Morris ....Knife Edge (1986)

Natalie J Robb .... Sheila Macintosh ....Violent Delights (1992)

Cathy Shipton .... Sarah Price ....Devil's Advocate (1995)

Gray O'Brien .... Det. Con. Rob Gibson.....Forbidden Fruit (1994)

.... Hellfire (1994)

Dougray Scott .... Colin Murphy....................Nest of Vipers (1992)

Sharon Small .... Michelle Gibson ....Forbidden Fruit (1994)

Michael Troughton............ Derek Halliday .... Out of Bounds (1997)

Paul Young .... Colin Davidson ....Funeral Rites (1987)

Gary Webster.................... Det.Sgt. Tilling ....Evil Eye (1990)

Greg Wise......................... Gregg Martin.............................. Hellfire (1994)

SCOTTISH NAMES FOR THE DEVIL

The Man o' France

Auld Nick

Auld Hornie

Auld Clootie

Domhnull Dubh / Black Donald

FAMILY REPUTATIONS

The sturdy Armstrongs

The trusty Boyds

The crooked Campbells

The greedy Campbells

The dirty Dalrymples

The doughty Douglases

The lucky Duffs

The dirty Dunbars

The bauld Frasers

The gallant / proud Grahams

The gay Gordons

The haughty Hamiltons

The handsome Hays

The hard rackle Homes

The gentle Johnstones

The crabbed Kerrs

The copper-nosed Kerrs

The skrae-skankit Laidlaws

The lightsome Lindsays

The brave Macdonalds

The Mackintoshes, fiery and
quick-tempered

The luckless Macleans

The proud MacNeils

The black Macraes o' Kintail	The proud Pringles
The manly Morrisons	The bold Rutherfords
The fause Monteiths	The red wud Ridderfords
The muckle-mou'd Murrays	The Setons, tall and proud
The windy Murrays	The strait-laced Sommervilles
The hard-headed Olivers	The lousy Turnbulls

THE SEA, THE SEA
Did you know ... ?

Due to a peculiarity of the topography of the estuary of the Firth of Forth, the coast between Alloa and Culross has twice the normal number of tides each day.

50 SCOTTISH PLACENAMES
THAT ARE HARDER TO PRONOUNCE
THAN AUCHTERMUCHTY

The following selection has been made at random. They are not necessarily the most difficult Scottish placenames to pronounce. Once you have worked out how to say them individually, try reading through the list at speed...

Abhainnsuidhe	Auchlunachan
Achadh Cheanathaidh	Badluchrach
Achadh Innis Chalainn	Bail Iochdrach
Achlorachan	Beinn a' Bhuchanaich
Achluachrach	Blarmachfoldach
Achnachluachrach	Bruach an Fhaslaghairt
Achnaphubuil	Bruichladdich
Achosnich	Clachan Dubhthaich
Achriabhach	Cladach Chirceboist
Airidh a'Bhruaich	Cladach Iolaraigh
Altnacaillich	Creaguaineach Loch
Ardchiavaig	Garadheancal
Ardchrishnish	Gobernuisgeach
Arinacrinachd	Gualachulain

Iverghiusachan Poit
Inverquhomery
Kilchallumkille
Kilconquhar
Killinochonoch
Kinlochlaich
Kinlochluichart
Knockchoilum
Leath Dail nan Cliabh
Loch a Ghainmhich
Loch Bheannchair

Loch Luichart
Lochtreighead
Mullach an Leathaid Riabhaich
Niachdaidh
Pitconnoquhoy
Rubh' Aird an Droighinn
Suidhe Cheanathaidh
Suidhe Chreunain
Timsgearraidh
Tolastadh a'Chaolais
Torrlaoighseach

WEATHER PREDICTIONS AND SAYINGS

Mony haws, mony snaws.

A frosty winter, a dusty March, a rain about April,
Another about the Lammas time when the corn begins to fill,
Is worth a pleuch o' gowd, and a' her pins theretill.

A misty May and a dropping June
Brings the bonny land o' Moray aboon.

E'ening red an' morning grey,
Is a taiken o' a bonny day;
E'ening grey an' morning red,
Put on your hat or you'll wet your head.

Ne'er cast a clout till May is out.

Gin Candlemas day be dry and fair,
The half o' Winter's to come and mair.
Gin Candlemas day be wet and foul,
The half o' Winter's gone at Youl

When March comes in with an adder's head, it goes out with a peacock's tail;
When it comes in with a peacock's tail, it goes out with an adder's head.
When the wind is in the North, hail comes forth,
When the wind is in the West, look for a wet blast;
When the wind is in the Soud, the weather will be fresh and good,
When the wind is in the East, cauld and snaw comes niest.

PERSONAL REMARKS, COMPLIMENTARY AND OTHERWISE

There is a rich store of evocative phrases to be found in day-to-day speech in various parts of Scotland that refer to personal appearance and characteristics. The following list is by no means comprehensive.

ba' heid   *noun*. A term of address, indicating that the person addressed is, in the opinion of the speaker, foolish or in error. Insult.

bampot   *noun*. A mad, crazy, foolish or eccentric person. Insult. (Used in some contexts, especially by another 'bampot', this word may indicate a hint of admiration.)

clarty   *adjective*. A term used to describe a person who is dirty, in appearance, habit, thought – or all three. Also, richt clarty. Insult.

dim light   *noun phrase*. 'He/she looks better in dim light'. Insult.

ferry-louper   *noun*. A term used by island-dwellers to refer to incomers from the mainland.

glaikit   *adjective*. used to describe a person who has not been blessed with the brains of a great thinker. Insult – which may be said with a kindly shake of the head.

hackit   *adjective*, used to describe someone who has not been blessed with great beauty. Insult.

nip or nippy   *adjective*. 'He/she is awfy nippy or he/she nips ma heid (head)': He/she is very irritating. Insult.

midden   *noun*. 'He/she is dressed like a midden': He/she lacks fashion sense. Insult.

manky   *adjective*. Referring to a person or thing that is lacking in hygiene and could potentially be **mingin'**. Insult.

mingin'   *adjective*. Used to describe a person who is unattractive, possibly offending the nose, the eye and one's respect for hygiene. Insult.

mockit   *adjective*. Used to describe a person who has little regard for personal cleanliness. Insult.

numpty   *noun*. Someone who could also be described as **glaikit** (qv). Insult.

nyaff   *noun*. An annoying person of diminutive stature: 'That bampot's nothing but a wee nyaff.' Insult.

Sassenach   *adjective*. a Gaelic term used by people in the Highlands to refer to a lowland Scot. Also sometimes used by the Scots to describe the English. [Bizarrely, it comes from the Anglo-Saxon for 'Saxon'.]

stoater   *noun*. A term used to describe an attractive person. Compliment – frequently used ironically.

teuchter   *noun*. A term used by people in Central Scotland to refer to people from the Highlands and Islands.

tumshie   *noun*. Turnip. Also tumshie-heid, turnip head. A term of address, indicating that the person who is being addressed is, in the opinion of the speaker, intellectually challenged. Insult.

He or she has a face like a:

guiser's neep	a Halloween turnip lantern. Insult
Halloween cake	not blessed with a subtle beauty. Insult.
meltit welly	a melted wellington boot. Insult.
skittery hippen	a dirty nappy. Use your imagination. Insult.
torn scone/torn melodian	having an unhappy/discontented appearance. Statement of perceived fact.
weel-skelpit erse	a well-smacked bottom. He/she is of ruddy complexion. Insult.

TO BOLDLY GO:
SCOTS EXPLORERS, ADVENTURERS AND PROMINENT FIGURES ABROAD

William Balfour Baikie (1825–64)	Explored the Rover Niger and opened it for navigation.
David Douglas (1799–1834)	Botanist and plant collector who travelled widely, particularly in north America. Best remembered for the Douglas Fir, which he introduced to Britain.
Alexander Duff (1806–78)	Devoted his life to missionary work in India.
Thomas Blake Glover (1838–1911)	Established himself as a trader in weapons and ships in Japan and played a major role in the industrialisation of the country.
Samuel Greig (1735–88)	Born in Inverkeithing and travelled to Russia and carried out major reforms in the Russian Naval Service. Catherine

the Great appointed him Supreme Admiral of the Russian Navy.

David Livingstone (1819–73)
Initially travelled to Africa as a missionary and returned, first to explore the Zambesi River and then to track the Nile to its source. Discovered Lake Ngami and the Victoria Falls.

John Alexander Macdonald (1815–91)
Emigrated to Canada in 1820. Became the first Prime Minister of the Confederation in 1867. Served 1867–1873 and again 1878–1891.

Alexander Mackenzie (1822–92)
Emigrated to Canada in 1842. Served as the first Liberal Prime Minister of Canada, 1873–1878.

Lachlan Macquarie (1761–1824)
After military service in North America, Egypt and India, he served very succesfully as governor of New South Wales. MacQuarie Island, the Macquarie River and the Lachlan River are named after him.

Mungo Park (1771–1806)
Explorer in Africa. Embarked on two expeditions to track the course of the river Niger and was killed on the second expedition before he reached the source.

Alan Pinkerton (1819–84)
Emigrated to America in 1842 and founded the Pinkerton Detective Agency in Chicago (1850). A pioneer in the field of federal intelligence and security.

James Ramsay (1733–96)
Served as a pastor on the island of St Christopher in the Caribbean. On his return to Great Britain, he campaigned vigorously against the slave trade.

Mary Slessor (1848–1915)
A mill worker who trained for the missions before travelling to Calabar, Nigeria in 1876. Devoted the rest of her life to working with the people there.

John McDougall Stuart (1816–66)
Made several expeditions to Australia. First to cross Australia from south to

John Witherspoon (1723-94)

north (1862) Mount Stuart is named after him.

A Paisley minister who emigrated to America in 1768. Served as president of the College of New Jersey, represented the state at the Continental Congress of 1776-82 and signed the American Declaration of Independence in 1776.

SCOTTISH FISHING BOAT REGISTRATION CODES

It is a legal requirement for fishing boats to be registered at a recognized port of registry. Registration details include the date of construction of the boat, the owner, the tonnage, etc. The numbers painted on the sides of fishing boats are registration numbers. The letter, or letters, indicate the port at which they are registered. The following list gives the letter code for each Scottish port of registration.

Aberdeen – A

Alloa – AA

Ardrossan – AD

Ayr – AR

Ballantrae – BA

Banff – BF

Bo'ness – BO

Broadford - BRD

Buckie – BCK

Burntisland – BU

Campbeltown – CN

Castlebay – CY

Dumfries – DS

Dundee – DE

Fraserburgh – FR

Glasgow – GW

Grangemouth – GH

Granton – GN

Greenock – GK

Inverness – INS

Irvine – IE

Kirkcaldy – KY

Kirkwall – K

Leith – LH

Lerwick – LK

Methil – ML

Montrose – ME

Oban – OB

Peterhead – PD

Rothesay – RO

Stornoway – SY

Stranraer – SR

Tarbert Loch Fyne – TT

Troon – TN

Ullapool – UL

Wick – WK

Wigtown – WN

DIOCESES OF THE ROMAN CATHOLIC CHURCH IN SCOTLAND

Glasgow
St Andrews and Edinburgh
Aberdeen
Argyll and the Isles

Dunkeld
Galloway
Motherwell
Paisley

DIOCESES OF THE SCOTTISH EPISCOPAL CHURCH

Aberdeen and Orkney
Argyll and the Isles
Brechin
Edinburgh

Glasgow and Galloway
Moray, Ross and Caithness
St Andrews, Dunkeld and Dunblane

PRESBYTERIES OF THE CHURCH OF SCOTLAND

Edinburgh
West Lothian
Lothian
Melrose and Peebles
Duns
Jedburgh
Annandale and Eskdale
Dumfries and Kirkcudbright
Wigtown and Stranraer
Ayr
Irvine and Kilmarnock
Ardrossan
Lanark
Paisley
Greenock
Glasgow
Hamilton
Dumbarton
South Argyll

Dunoon
Lorn and Mull
Falkirk
Stirling
Dunfermline
Kirkcaldy
St Andrews
Dunkeld and Meigle
Perth
Dundee
Angus
Aberdeen
Kincardine and Deeside
Gordon
Buchan
Moray
Abernethy
Inverness
Lochaber

Ross
Sutherland
Caithness
Lochcarron – Skye
Uist
Lewis

Orkney
Shetland
England
Europe
Jerusalem

PRESBYTERIES OF THE UNITED FREE CHURCH OF SCOTLAND

Presbytery of the East (Fife, the Lothians, the Borders and Stirlingshire)
Presbytery of the West (Lanarkshire, Ayrshire, Renfrewshire,
Dunbartonshire and Glasgow
Presbytery of the North (Perthshire, North Fife, Angus, Grampians,
Highlands and Islands)

PRESBYTERIES OF THE FREE CHURCH OF SCOTLAND

Northern
Inverness, Lochaber and Ross
Western Isles

Edinburgh and Perth
Glasgow and Argyll
Skye and Wester Ross

SCOTTISH CONGREGATIONS OF THE FREE PRESBYTERIAN CHURCH OF SCOTLAND

Aberdeen
Edinburgh
Glasgow
Fort William
Perth
Highlands: Kyle of Lochalsh,
Lochcarron, Applecross, Shieldaig,
Gairloch, Laide, Ullapool, Lochinver,
Stoer, Scourie, Kinlochbervie,

Halkirk, Bonar Bridge, Dornoch,
Dingwall, Beauly, Inverness, Farr,
Strathkerrick, Tomatin
Western Isles and Skye: North
Uist, Leverburgh, Tarbert, Uig,
Breasdete, Ness, North Tolsta,
Stornoway, Achmore, Staffin,
Portree, Raasay, Broadford, Struan,
Vatten, Glendale

THE FILMS OF SIR SEAN CONNERY, FROM 1956–2006

1956 .... No Road Back	1977 .... A Bridge Too Far
1957 .....Requiem for a Heavyweight	1979 .... Meteor
1957 .... Hell Drivers	1979 .... Cuba
(also known as Hard Drivers)	1979 .... The Great Train Robbery
1957 ....Time Lock	1981 .... Time Bandits
1957 ....Action of the Tiger	1981 .... Outland
1958 ... Another Time Another Place	1982 .... Wrong Is Right
1959 .... Darby O'Gill and the Little	1982 .... Five Days One Summer
.... People	1982 ....Sword of the Valiant
1959 .... Tarzan's Greatest Adventure	1983 Never Say Never Again
1961 ....The Frightened City	1986 .... Highlander
1961 Operation Snafu / On the Fiddle	1986 .... Name of the Rose
1962 .... The Longest Day	1987 ....The Untouchables
1962 ....Dr No	1988 ....The Presidio
1963 ....From Russia With Love	1988 ....Memories of Me
1964 .... Goldfinger	1989 ....Indiana Jones and the Last
1964 .... Woman of Straw	....Crusade
1964 .... Marnie	1989 .... Family Business
1965 .... The Hill	1990 ...... The Hunt for Red October
1965 ....Thunderball	1990 .... The Russia House
1966 .... A Fine Madness	1991 Robin Hood, Prince of Thieves
1967 .... You Only Live Twice	1991 ....Highlander II
1968 .... Shalako	1992 ....Medicine Man
1970 ....The Molly Maguires	1993 ....Rising Sun
1971 .... The Red Tent	1994 .... A Good Man in Africa
1971 ....The Anderson Tapes	1995 ....Just Cause
1971 .... Diamonds are Forever	1995 ....First Knight
1973 .... The Offence	1996 .... Dragonheart
1974 .... Zardoz	1996 .... The Rock
1974 . Murder on the Orient Express	1998 ....The Avengers
1974 ....The Terrorists	1998 .... Playing by Heart
1975 ....The Wind and the Lion	1999 .... Entrapment
1975 The Man Who Would Be King	2000 .... Finding Forrester
1975 ....Ransom	2003 ....The League of Extraordinary
1976 ....Robin and Marion	..................................Gentlemen
1976 .... The Next Man	2006 ....Sir Billi the Vet

THE CONSISTENT APPROACH TO FOREIGN ACCENTS OF SIR SEAN CONNERY

Sean Connery, as well as being famous throughout most of his career as being Scotland's sexiest actor, with a working life spanning over fifty years, generous donations to the Scottish National Party and having the world's most admired and famous balding head, is also famous for the admirable philosophy that an actor shouldn't have to put on an accent just to make a part believable.

The theory that he might just not be very good at accents is not one we would choose to accept here. Below is a selection of parts where Sir Sean could have attempted an accent but chose not to (with the exception of The Untouchables where a discernable Irish twang does creep into his performance for some of the film).

Year	Film	Character	Accent not attempted
1975	Ransom	Nils Tahlvik	Norwegian
1975	The Wind and the Lion	Mulay Achmed Mohammed el-Raisuli the Magnificent	Arabian
1976	Robin and Marion	Robin Hood	English
1976	The Next Man	Khalil Abdul-Muhsen	Arabian
1981	The Time Bandits	King Agamemnon	Ancient Greek
1986	Highlander	Juan Sanchez Villa-Lobos Ramirez	Spanish (though he claims to have been born in Egypt)
1987	The Untouchables	Jim Malone	Irish
1990	Hunt for Red October	Captain Marko Ramius	Russian
1991	Highlander II	Juan Sanchez Villa-Lobos Ramirez	Spanish (though in this sequel it turns out he is from the planet Zeist)
1991	Robin Hood Prince of Thieves	King Richard the Lionheart	English
1995	First Knight	King Arthur	English
1996	Dragonheart	Draco	Dragonian?

LOCATIONS OF ST ANDREWS SOCIETIES AROUND THE WORLD

Argentina............................1 society

Australia ....1 society

Brazil ....1 society

Canada...............7 societies (Calgary, Montreal, Ontario, Ottawa, St John, Toronto, Winnipeg)

China.............1 society (Hong Kong)

Denmark.............................1 society

Gibraltar ....1 society

Indonesia.............................1 society

Ireland   ....1 society

Malaysia................................1 society

Mexico ....1 society

Netherlands ....1 society

Russia ....1 society

Scotland ....3 societies (Aberdeen, Edinburgh, Glasgow)

Singapore ....1 society

Thailand ....1 society

USA:

Alabama...............................4 societies

Alaska....................................1 society

California ....7 societies

Colorado ....1 society

Connecticut...........................1 society

Florida..................................7 societies

Georgia...............................3 societies

Hawaii ....1 society

Illinois ....2 societies

Indiana ....1 society

Kansas ....2 societies

Louisiana ....2 societies

Maine ....1 society

Maryland ....3 societies

Massachusetts ....2 societies

Michigan ....2 societies

Minnesota ....2 societies

Missouri ....2 societies

Nevada ....1 society

New Hampshire ....1 society

New Mexico ....1 society

New York ....5 societies

North Carolina ....2 societies

North Dakota ....1 society

Ohio ....1 society

Oregon ....1 society

Pennsylvania ....3 societies

Rhode Island ....1 society

South Carolina ....1 society

Tennessee ....1 society

Vermont ....1 society

Virginia ....3 societies

Washington ....2 societies

Washington DC ....1 society

Wisconsin ....1 society

LESSER-KNOWN SPORTS AND GAMES ORGANISATIONS OF SCOTLAND

Chess Scotland (Amalgamation of the Scottish Chess Association and the Scottish Junior Chess Association

The Falkland Palace Real Tennis Club

The Grampian Speleological Club
The Scottish Canoe Association
The Scottish Clay Target Association
The Scottish Croquet Association
The Scottish Cyclists Union
The Scottish Draughts Association
The Scottish Ferret Club
The Scottish Hang Gliding and Paragliding
    Federation
The Scottish Homing Union (Racing Pigeons)
The Scottish Orienteering Association
The Scottish Petanque Association
The Scottish Quoiting Association
The Scottish Sport Parachute Organisation
The Scottish Scrabble League
The Scottish Stamper's Club
The Scottish Tiddlywinks Association (ScotTwA)

LESSER KNOWN CRAFT, HOBBY AND SPECIAL INTEREST ORGANISATIONS IN SCOTLAND

Scotswood (Scottish chapter of the Association of
    Woodturners of Great Britain)
The Association of Scottish Philatelic Societies
The Embroiderers Guild Scotland
The Gaddgedlar Historical Re-enactment Society
The Marquetry Society Scottish Group
The Scottish Aeromodeller's Association
The Scottish Aviation Network (plane spotting)
The Scottish Brewing Archive (real ale)
The Scottish Machine Knitting Association
The Scottish Military Vehicle Club
The Scottish Railway Preservation Society
The Scottish Science Fiction Confederation
The Scottish Society of Amateur Artists
The Scottish Stampers Club
The Scottish Traction Engine Society

The Scottish Vintage Vehicle Federation
The Thimble Guild (aka Scotland Direct)
Thistle Quilters
The West of Scotland Military Modelling Group
The William Topaz McGonagall Appreciation
Society

WEE WILLIE WINKIE
By William Miller (1810–1872)

Wee Willie Winkie rins through the toun,
Upstairs and doonstairs in his nicht goun,
Tirlin' at the window, cryin' at the lock,
'Are the weans in their beds, for it's noo ten
o'clock?'
'Hey, Willie Winkie, are ye comin' ben?
The cat's singin' grey thrums to the sleepin' hen,
The dog's spelder'd on the floor, and disnae gie a
cheep,
But here's a waukrife laddie that winna fa' asleep!
'Onything but sleep, ye rogue! glowerin' like the
moon,
Rattlin' in an airn jug wi' an airn spoon,
Rumblin', tumblin' round about, crawin' like a
cock,
Skirlin' like a kenna-whit, waulk'nin' sleepin' folk.
'Hey, Willie Winkie – the wean's in a creel!
Wamblin' aff a bodie's knee like a verra eel,
Ruggin' at the cat's lug, and ravelin' a' her
thrums—
Hey, Willie Winkie – see, there he comes!'
Wearit is the mither that has a stoorie wean,
A wee stumpie stoussie, that canna rin his lane,
That has a battle aye wi' sleep before he'll close
an ee—
But a kiss frae aff his rosy lips gies strength anew
tae me.

EXTRACTS FROM THE WORK OF
WILLIAM TOPAZ McGONAGALL (*c.*1825–1902)

The Ancient Town of Leith

Ancient town of Leith, most wonderful to
    be seen,
With your many handsome buildings, and
    lovely links so green,
And the first buildings I may mention are
    the Courthouse and Town Hall,
Also Trinity House, and the Sailors' Home
    of Call.

Then as for Leith Fort, it was erected in
    1779, which is really grand,
And which is now the artillery headquarters
    in Bonnie Scotland;
And as for the Docks, they are magnificent
    to see,
They comprise five docks, two piers, 1,141
    yards long respectively.

The Newport Railway

Success to the Newport Railway,
Along the braes of the Silvery Tay,
And to Dundee straightway,
Across the Railway Bridge o' the Silvery
    Tay,
Which was opened on the 12th of May,
In the year of our Lord 1879,
Which will clear all expenses in a very short
    time
Because the thrifty housewives of Newport
To Dundee will often resort,
Which will be to them profit and sport,
By bringing cheap tea, bread, and jam,
And also some of Lipton's ham,

Which will make their hearts feel light
   and gay,
And cause them to bless the opening day
Of the Newport Railway.

DOH!
Did you know ...?

Homer Simpson's catchphrase 'DOH!' was based on the catchphrase of actor James Finlayson who was born in Falkirk in 1887 and starred alongside Laurel and Hardy in many of their films.

THE DECLARATION OF
ARBROATH, 1320

In 1314 Robert the Bruce and his army soundly defeated the English at Bannockburn but wars with England continued. Robert Bruce had been excommunicated by Pope John XXII following Bruce's murder of a rival on the steps of a Franciscan Priory. Encouraged by the propaganda of the English king, the Pope also excommunicated the whole of Scotland. The Pope's alliance with the English king was in order to gain support for another Crusade to the Holy Land.

The *Declaration of Arbroath*, one of the most famous documents in Scotland's history, is a plea sent to Pope John XXII in the form of a letter, to acknowledge the independence of Scotland, attempting to counter English propaganda. Written in Latin, submitted and signed by eight earls and thirty-one Scottish nobles on April 6, 1320, it is believed to have been drafted by Bernard de Linton, the Abbot of Arbroath, Chancellor of Scotland.

While the Declaration stated that a new King of Scots would be chosen if Robert the Bruce did not support the independence of Scotland, this was done in the knowledge that there was no one else to take his place, in other words: a bluff. Some argue that the declaration is merely a diplomatic document, the intention of which was to appease the Pope, others say that it is a true declaration of desire for independence.

Scotland remained excommunicated, but it was in part as a result of the

Pope's intervention that on March 1, 1328, a treaty between Scotland and England, renouncing English claims to Scotland, was signed by Edward III.

The document is the first formal declaration of independence by any nation, and it was used as a model for the American Declaration of Independence. April 6 has been adopted, in America, as Tartan Day.

Signatories

Duncan, Earl of Fife
Thomas Randolph, Earl of Moray, Lord of Man and of Annandale
Patrick Dunbar, Earl of March
Malise, Earl of Strathearn
Malcolm, Earl of Lennox
William, Earl of Ross
Magnus, Earl of Caithness and Orkney
William, Earl of Sutherland
Walter, Steward of Scotland
William Soules, Butler of Scotland
James, Lord of Douglas
Roger Mowbray
David, Lord of Brechin
David Graham
Ingram Umfraville
John Menteith, guardian of the earldom of Menteith
Alexander Fraser
Gilbert Hay, Constable of Scotland
Robert Keith, Marischal of Scotland
Henry St Clair
John Graham
David Lindsay
William Oliphant
Patrick Graham
John Fenton
William Abernethy
David Wemyss
William Mushet
Fergus of Ardrossan
Eustace Maxwell
William Ramsay

William Mowat
Alan Murray
Donald Campbell
John Cameron
Reginald Cheyne
Alexander Seton
Andrew Leslie
Alexander Straiton

Some additional names were inscribed on some of the seal tags. Seven of them were legible:

John Durrant
Alexander Lamberton
Edward Keith
John Inchman
Thomas Menzies
Thomas Marham

The Declaration of Arbroath

Letter of Barons of Scotland to Pope John XXII

'To the Most Holy Father in Christ and Lord, the Lord John, by divine providence Supreme Pontiff of the Holy Roman and Universal Church, his humble and devout sons Duncan, Earl of Fife, Thomas Randolph, Earl of Moray, Lord of Man and of Annandale, Patrick Dunbar, Earl of March, Malise, Earl of Strathearn, Malcolm, Earl of Lennox, William, Earl of Ross, Magnus, Earl of Caithness and Orkney, and William, Earl of Sutherland; Walter, Steward of Scotland, William Soules, Butler of Scotland, James, Lord of Douglas, Roger Mowbray, David, Lord of Brechin, David Graham, Ingram Umfraville, John Menteith, guardian of the earldom of Menteith, Alexander Fraser, Gilbert Hay, Constable of Scotland, Robert Keith, Marischal of Scotland, Henry St Clair, John Graham, David Lindsay, William Oliphant, Patrick Graham, John Fenton, William Abernethy, David Wemyss, William Mushet, Fergus of Ardrossan, Eustace Maxwell, William Ramsay, William Mowat, Alan Murray, Donald Campbell, John Cameron, Reginald Cheyne, Alexander Seton, Andrew Leslie, and Alexander Straiton, and the other barons and freeholders and the whole commity of the realm of Scotland send all manner of filial reverence, with devout kisses of his blessed feet.

'Most Holy Father and Lord, we know and from the chronicles and books of the ancients we find that among other famous nations our own, the Scots, has been graced with widespread renown. They journeyed from Greater Scythia by way of the Tyrrhenian Sea and the Pillars of Hercules, and dwelt for a long course of time in Spain among the most savage tribes, but nowhere could they be subdued by any race, however barbarous. Thence they came, twelve hundred years after the people of Israel crossed the Red Sea, to their home in the west where they still live today. The Britons they first drove out, the Picts they utterly destroyed, and, even though very often assailed by the Norwegians, the Danes and the English, they took possession of that home with many victories and untold efforts; and, as the historians of old time bear witness, they have held it free of all bondage ever since. In their kingdom there have reigned one hundred and thirteen kings of their own royal stock, the line unbroken by a single foreigner.

'The high qualities and deserts of these people, were they not otherwise manifest, gain glory enough from this: that the King of kings and Lord of lords, our Lord Jesus Christ, after His Passion and Resurrection, called them, even though settled in the uttermost parts of the earth, almost the first to His most holy faith. Nor would He have them confirmed in that faith by merely anyone but by the first of His Apostles by calling – though second or third in rank – the most gentle Saint Andrew, the Blessed Peter's brother, and desired him to keep them under his protection as their patron for ever.

'The Most Holy Fathers your predecessors gave careful heed to these things and bestowed many favours and numerous privileges on this same kingdom and people, as being the special charge of the Blessed Peter's brother. Thus our nation under their protection did indeed live in freedom and peace up to the time when that mighty prince the King of the English, Edward, the father of the one who reigns today, when our kingdom had no head and our people harboured no malice or treachery and were then unused to wars or invasions, came in the guise of a friend and ally to harass them as an enemy. The deeds of cruelty, massacre, violence, pillage, arson, imprisoning prelates, burning down monasteries, robbing and killing monks and nuns, and yet other outrages without number which he committed against our people, sparing neither age nor sex, religion nor rank, no one could describe nor fully imagine unless he had seen them with his own eyes.

'But from these countless evils we have been set free, by the help of Him who though He afflicts yet heals and restores, by our most tireless Prince, King and Lord, the Lord Robert. He, that his people and his heritage might be delivered out of the hands of our enemies, met toil and fatigue, hunger and peril, like another Maccabaeus or Joshua, and bore them cheerfully. Him, too, divine providence, his right of succession according to our laws and customs which we shall maintain to the death, and the due consent and assent of us all have made our Prince and

King. To him, as to the man by whom salvation has been wrought unto our people, we are bound both by law and by his merits that our freedom may be still maintained, and by him, come what may, we mean to stand.

'Yet if he should give up what he has begun, and agree to make us or our kingdom subject to the King of England or the English, we should exert ourselves at once to drive him out as our enemy and a subverter of his own rights and ours, and make some other man who was well able to defend us our King; for, as long as but a hundred of us remain alive, never will we on any conditions be brought under English rule. It is in truth not for glory, nor riches, nor honours that we are fighting, but for freedom – for that alone, which no honest man gives up but with life itself.

'Therefore it is, Reverend Father and Lord, that we beseech your Holiness with our most earnest prayers and suppliant hearts, inasmuch as you will in your sincerity and goodness consider all this, that, since with Him Whose vice-gerent on earth you are there is neither weighing nor distinction of Jew and Greek, Scotsman or Englishman, you will look with the eyes of a father on the troubles and privations brought by the English upon us and upon the Church of God. May it please you to admonish and exhort the King of the English, who ought to be satisfied with what belongs to him since England used once to be enough for seven kings or more, to leave us Scots in peace, who live in this poor Scotland, beyond which there is no dwelling-place at all, and covet nothing but our own. We are sincerely willing to do anything for him, having regard to our condition, that we can to win peace for ourselves.

'This truly concerns you, Holy Father, since you see the savagery of the heathen raging against the Christians, as the sins of Christians have indeed deserved, and the frontiers of Christendom being pressed inward every day; and how much it will tarnish your Holiness's memory if (which God forbid) the Church suffers eclipse or scandal in any branch of it during your time, you must perceive. Then rouse the Christian princes who for false reasons pretend that they cannot go to the help of the Holy Land because of wars they have on hand with their neighbours. The real reason that prevents them is that in making war on their smaller neighbours they find quicker profit and weaker resistance. But how cheerfully our Lord the King and we too would go there if the King of the English would leave us in peace, He from Whom nothing is hidden well knows; and we profess and declare it to you as the Vicar of Christ and to all Christendom.

'But if your Holiness puts too much faith in the tales the English tell and will not give sincere belief to all this, nor refrain from favouring them to our prejudice, then the slaughter of bodies, the perdition of souls, and all other misfortunes that will follow, inflicted by them on us and by us on them, will, we believe, be surely laid by the Most High to your charge.

'To conclude we are and shall ever be, as far as duty calls us, ready to do your will in all things, as obedient sons to you as His Vicar; and to Him as the Supreme King and Judge we commit the maintenance of our cause, casting our cares upon Him and firmly trusting that He will inspire us with courage and bring our enemies to nought.

'May the Most High preserve you to His Holy Church in holiness and health and grant you length of days.

'Given at the monastery of Arbroath in Scotland on the sixth day of the month of April in the year of grace thirteen hundred and twenty and the fifteenth year of the reign of our King aforesaid.'

© *Crown copyright. Located in the National Archives of Scotland, Edinburgh.*

GIRLS' AND BOYS' NAMES: THE TOP TWENTY, 2007–2008

Boys 2007		Girls 2007	
1	Lewis	1	Sophie
2	Jack	2	Emma
3	Ryan	3	Lucy
4	James	4	Katie
5	Callum	5	Erin
6	Cameron	6	Ellie
7	Daniel	7	Amy
8	Liam	8	Emily
9=	Jamie	9	Chloe
9=	Kyle	10	Olivia
9=	Matthew	11	Hannah
12	Logan	12	Jessica
13	Finlay	13	Grace
14	Adam	14	Ava
15	Alexander	15	Rebecca
16	Dylan	16	Isla
17	Aiden	17	Brooke
18	Andrew	18	Megan
19	Ben	19	Niamh
20=	Aaron	20	Eilidh
20=	Connor		

Boys 2008		Girls 2008	
1	Jack	1	Sophie
2	Lewis	2	Emily
3	Daniel	3	Olivia
4	Liam	4	Chloe
5=	James	5	Emma
5=	Ryan	6	Lucy
7	Callum	7	Ava
8	Logan	8	Katie
9	Matthew	9	Erin
10	Cameron	10	Hannah
11	Alexander	11	Ellie
12=	Aiden	12	Jessica
12=	Dylan	13	Amy
14	Aaron	14	Isla
15	Ben	15	Grace
16	Kyle	16	Eva
17	Jamie	17	Rebecca
18	Finlay	18	Leah
19	Adam	19	Freya
20	Andrew	20	Holly

BAD LUCK

According to Scots superstitious belief, it is unlucky to:

- Lay a baby down for its first sleep in a new crib
- Place new shoes on the table
- Cut young babies' nails with scissors (it makes them dishonest)
- Take pigs on fishing boats, or mention pigs on fishing boats
- Be first-footed by a fair-haired or flat-footed person
- Cross two knives on the table
- See a funeral procession or a pig on the way to your wedding
- Have a black cat in a room where a wake is being held

GOOD LUCK

According to traditional belief in Scotland, it is lucky to:

- Have a rowan tree outside your house (it keeps witches at bay)
- Place silver in a new baby's hand (to bring wealth in later life)
- Touch iron if you see or hear evil

- Put a silver coin in your shoe if you are a bride
- Wear a sprig of white heather (frowned upon nowadays for ecological reasons)

IMPORTANT BATTLES
FOUGHT BY SCOTS

84 AD	Mons Graupius	An army of Roman legionaries and auxiliaries under Agricola defeated a large force of Caledonian Picts, led by Calgacus.
937	Brunanburh	A combined force of Scots (led by Constantine II), Strathclyde Britons (led by Owin) and Norsemen (led by Olaf) were defeated by an English army under Aethelstan.
1018	Carham	Malcolm II, supported by Owin of Strathclyde, defeated Adulf Cadel, Earl of Northumbria.
1040	Pitgaveney	Macbeth secured a victory over the army of Duncan I, who was killed.
1057	Lumphanan	Macbeth was slain in battle with Malcolm, son of Duncan I.
1093	Alnwick	The Scots, led by Malcolm III, were attacked and defeated while besieging Alnwick. Malcolm III was killed.
August 22, 1138	Northallerton	The Scots, led by David I, were heavily defeated by an English army assembled by Thurstan, Archbishop of York. This was the battle of the Standards.
1174	Alnwick	William I, attempting to succeed where Malcolm III had failed, attacks Alnwick, is defeated and captured.

1263	Largs	A force led by King Haakon of Norway was forced into retreat by the Scots under Alexander III.
September 11, 1297	Stirling Bridge	William Wallace led an army to victory against the English led by John de Warrenne, Earl of Surrey.
July 22, 1298	Falkirk	Scots led By William Wallace were defeated by the English under Edward I.
June 18, 1306	Methven	An English force led by Aymer de Valence, Earl of Pembroke, defeated Bruce's army after taking them by surprise
May 10, 1307	Loudon Hill	The Scots led by Robert the Bruce defeated an English army led by Aymer de Valence.
June 24, 1314	Bannockburn	The English army of Edward II was defeated by the Scots, led by Robert the Bruce.
August 12, 1332	Dupplin Moor	The Scots, led by the Earl of Mar, were defeated by an English army, led by Edward Balliol.
July 9, 1333	Halidon Hill	The Scots, led by Sir Archibald Douglas, were defeated by the English under the command of Edward III and Edward Balliol.
October 17, 1346	Neville's Cross	An English army, led by the Archbishop of York and Sir Henry Percy, defeated the Scots army and captured King David II.
August 19, 1388	Otterburn	The Scots defeated the English, led by Sir Henry Percy. In the course of the battle, the Scots leader, James Earl of Douglas, was killed.
September 13, 1402	Homildon Hill	The Scots, led by Archibald, 4th Earl of Douglas, were defeated by the English, led by Sir Henry Percy and the Earl of March.

June 11, 1488	Sauchieburn	James III was defeated by a force of rebellious nobles. The King was thrown from his horse and then stabbed to death by a priest.
September 9, 1513	Flodden	James IV led a large Scottish army into battle against the English under the command of the Earl of Surrey. The Scots were heavily defeated and James was killed.
November 24, 1542	Solway Moss	The Scots were routed by an small English army led by Lords Wharton and Musgrave. As a result, it is said that James V died of a broken heart.
February 25, 1545	Ancrum Moor	An English army led by Sir Ralph Eure (or Evers) was utterly defeated by the Scots, led by the Earl of Angus.
September 10, 1547	Pinkie Cleuch	The Duke of Somerset led the English against a large Scots army under the command of the Earl of Arran. The Scots force was completely destroyed.
May 13, 1568	Langside	The army of Mary, Queen of Scots was defeated by an army under the command of the Regent Moray.
September 1, 1644	Tippermuir	James Graham, Marquis of Montrose led a royalist army to victory against Covenanting forces under the command of Lord Elcho.
September 13, 1644	Aberdeen	The Marquis of Montrose led the Royalists to victory against Lord Burleigh's covenanting army.
February 2, 1645	Inverlochy	A heavily outnumbered royalist force led by James Graham, Marquis of Montrose, defeated an army of Covenanters led by Campbell of Glenlyon.
May 9, 1645	Auldearn	The Marquis of Montrose secured

		a victory for the royalists against an army led by Colonel Hurry.
July 2, 1645	Alford	The royalists under the Marquis of Montrose once more defeated the Covenanters, led by General Baillie.
August 15, 1645	Kilsyth	Montrose's royalist army annihilated the covenanting army led by General Baillie.
September 13, 1645	Philiphaugh	General David Leslie led a surprise attack on the tiny army of John Graham, Marquis of Montrose and massacred them.
September 3, 1650	Dunbar	Oliver Cromwell utterly defeated a large Scots army led by General David Leslie.
September 3, 1651	Worcester	A Scottish army, supporting the restoration of Charles II, is destroyed by Cromwell.
November 28, 1666	Rullion Green	A body of Galloway Covenanters was heavily defeated by a force led by Tam Dalziel.
June 1, 1679	Drumclog	A group of Covenanters defeated a larger force led by John Graham of Claverhouse. AKA Loudon Hill.
June 22, 1679	Bothwell Bridge	A force of Covenanters was defeated by a government army led by the Duke of Monmouth.
July 27, 1689	Killiecrankie	John Graham of Claverhouse led a Jacobite army to a bloody victory against General Mackay's army. Claverhouse fell in battle.
February 12, 1692	Glencoe	A group of Campbells, led by Campbell of Glenlyon and acting on a royal warrant, attacked their hosts, the Macdonalds of Glencoe, while they slept. More than forty of the Macdonald clan were killed.

November 13, 1715	Sheriffmuir	A Jacobite army, led by the Earl of Mar, fought with government troops under the Duke of Argyll. Both sides claimed victory.
June 10, 1719	Glenshiel	A Jacobite force under the Marquess of Tullibardine was confronted by a small government army and easily defeated.
September 21, 1745	Prestonpans	Charles Edward Stewart led the Jacobites to victory in a surprise attack on Sir John Cope's army.
January 23, 1746	Falkirk	The Jacobite army defeated a government army under the command of General Hawley.
April 16, 1746	Culloden Moor	The Jacobites under Bonnie Prince Charlie were destroyed by the army of the Duke of Cumberland in a bloody fight. Charles was forced to flee. This was the last battle fought on British soil.

SMOOTH TALKING
Did you know ... ?

William of Orange died soon after his horse stumbled on a molehill and he fell off. The Jacobites, who had naturally been delighted to hear the news of the king's demise, composed a toast in celebration of the elusive creature whose digging had caused William's death:

'To the wee gentleman in the black velvet jacket'.

SCOTTISH FOOTBALL CLUBS –
FOUNDING DATES, HOME GROUNDS

Aberdeen FC	1903	Pittodrie Stadium
Airdrie United FC	2002	Excelsior Stadium, Airdrie
Albion Rovers FC	1882	Cliftonhall Stadium, Coatbridge
Alloa Athletic FC	1883	Recreation Park, Clackmannan

Arbroath FC	1878	Gayfield Park, Arbroath
Ayr United FC	1910	Somerset Park, Ayr
Berwick Rangers FC	1881	Shielfield Park, Berwick
Brechin City FC	1906	Glebe Park, Brechin
Brora Rangers FC	1878	Dudgeon Park, Brora
Buckie Thistle FC	1889	Victoria Park, Buckie
Clachnacuddin FC	1886	Grant Street Park, Inverness
Clyde FC	1878	Broadwood Stadium, Cumbernauld
Cove Rangers FC	1922	Allan Park, Aberdeen
Cowdenbeath FC	1881	Central Park, Cowdenbeath
Deveronvale FC	1938	Princess Royal Park, Banff
Dumbarton FC	1872	Strathclyde Homes Stadium, Dumbarton
Dundee FC	1893	Dens Park, Dundee
Dundee United FC	1909	Tannadice Park, Dundee
Dunfermline Athletic FC	1885	East End Park, Dunfermline
East Fife FC	1903	Bayview Stadium, Methil
East Stirlingshire FC	1881	Ochilview Park, Stenhousemuir
Elgin City FC	1893	Borough Briggs, Elgin
Falkirk FC	1876	Falkirk Stadium, Falkirk
Forfar Athletic FC	1885	Station Park, Forfar
Forres Mechanics FC	1884	Mosset Park, Forres
Fort William FC	1984	Claggan Park, Fort William
Fraserburgh FC	1910	Bellslea Park, Fraserburgh
Glasgow Celtic FC	1888	Celtic Park, Glasgow
Glasgow Rangers FC	1873	Ibrox Stadium, Glasgow
Greenock Morton FC	1874	Cappielow Park, Greenock
Gretna 2008 FC	2008	Everholm Stadium, Annan,
Hamilton Academicals FC	1874	New Douglas Park, Hamilton
Heart of Midlothian FC	1874	Tynecastle Stadium, Edinburgh
Hibernian FC	1875	Easter Road Stadium, Edinburgh
Huntly FC	1928	Christie Park, Huntly
Inverness Caledonian Thistle FC	1994	Caledonian Stadium, Inverness
Inverurie Loco Works FC	1903	Harlaw Park, Inverurie
Keith FC	1919	Kynoch Park, Keith
Kilmarnock FC	1869	Rugby Park, Kilmarnock

Livingston FC (formerly Meadowbank Thistle)	1974	Almondvale Stadium, Livingston
Lossiemouth FC	1945	Grant Park, Lossiemouth
Montrose FC	1879	Links Park, Montrose
Motherwell FC	1886	Fir Park, Motherwell
Nairn County FC	1914	Station Park, Nairn
Partick Thistle FC	1876	Firhill Stadium, Glasgow
Peterhead FC	1867	Balmoor Stadium, Peterhead
Queen of the South FC	1919	Palmerston Park, Dumfries
Queen's Park FC	1867	Hampden Park, Glasgow
Raith Rovers FC	1883	Stark's Park, Kirkcaldy
Ross County FC	1929	Victoria Park, Dingwall
Rothes FC	1938	Mackessack Park, Rothes
St Johnstone FC	1884	McDiarmid Park, Perth
St Mirren FC	1877	St Mirren Park, Paisley
Stenhousemuir FC	1884	Ochilview Park, Stenhousemuir
Stirling Albion FC	1945	Forthbank Stadium, Stirling
Stranraer FC	1870	Stair Park, Stranraer
Wick Academy FC	1893	Harmsworth Park, Wick

FAMOUS SUPPORTERS
OF SCOTTISH FOOTBALL CLUBS

Aberdeen
Richard Gordon (Sportscene presenter)
Paul Lawrie (Open golf champion)
Donny Munro (lead singer of Runrig)

Dumbarton
David Byrne (lead singer of Talking Heads)
Hazel Irvine (TV presenter)

Dundee United
George Galloway (politician)

Lorraine Kelly (TV presenter)
Ricky Ross (Lead singer of Deacon Blue)

Heart of Midlothian
Rory Bremner (impressionist)
Nicky Campbell (TV presenter)
Ronnie Corbett (comedian)
Gavin Hastings (rugby player)
Steven Hendry (snooker player)
Alex Salmond (SNP MP, MSP, First Minister)
Ken Stott (actor)

Hibernian

Fish (lead singer of Marillion)
Bernard Gallacher (golfer)
Sandy Lyle (golfer)
Shirley Manson (lead singer of Garbage)
Margo MacDonald (MSP)
Gail Porter (TV presenter)
Ian Rankin (author)
Craig and Charlie Reid (The Proclaimers)
Dougray Scott (actor)
Grant Stott (presenter)
Irvine Welsh (author)

Celtic

Jackie Bird (newsreader)
Bono (lead singer of U2)
Rhona Cameron (comedian and TV presenter)
Michael Caton Jones (director)
Billy Connolly (comedian)
Adam Crozier (former FA chief exec)
Clare Grogan (singer/actress/TV presenter)
Fran Healy (lead singer of Travis)
John Higgins (snooker player)
Jim Kerr (lead singer of Simple Minds)
Martine MacCutcheon (actress)
Alan MacManus (footballer)
Charlie Nicholas (football pundit)
John Reid (MP)
Tony Roper (actor and writer)
Elaine C Smith (actress)
Sharleen Spiteri (lead singer of Texas)
Rod Stewart (singer)

Rangers

Kenneth Branagh (actor)
Andy Cameron (comedian)
Robert Carlyle (actor)
Robbie Coltrane (actor)
Graeme Dott (snooker player)
Eddie Irvin (racing driver)
James MacPherson (actor)
Nell McAndrew (model)
Alan McGhee (head of Creation Records)
Marti Pellow (lead singer of Wet Wet Wet)
Gary Player (golfer)
Gordon Ramsay (celebrity chef)
David Sneddon (singer)
Midge Ure (singer)
Jonathan Watson (writer and comedian)
Jim White (sports presenter)
Kirsty Young (newsreader)

Partick Thistle

Justin Currie (lead singer of Del Amitri)
Sir Alistair Burnett (former newsreader)

Raith Rovers

Gordon Brown (MP)
Jocky Wilson (darts player)

St Johnstone

Stuart Cosgrove (football pundit)
Fred MacAulay (comedian)
Ewan MacGregor (actor)

THE SCOTT MONUMENT – VITAL STATISTICS

- Location: Princes Street Gardens East, Edinburgh
- Architect: George Meikle Kemp (winning the design competition under the pseudonym John Morvo)
- Statue of Scott and his dog Maida designed by John Steel (Carrara marble)
- Style: Gothic – inspired by Melrose Abbey
- Building work commenced: 1840
- Height: 200 feet 6 inches (61.5 metres approx)
- Base measurement: 55 feet (14.5 metres approx) square
- Number of steps to top: 278
- Depth of Foundations: 52 feet (16 metres approx)
- Tower complete: 1844 (7 months after the death of Kemp)
- Statue unveiled: 1846
- The monument contains 64 statuettes representing characters in Scott's novels. The first eight were in place when the monument was completed. In 1871 a further 24 were added. The last 32 were in place by 1882.

THE WALLACE MONUMENT, STIRLING – VITAL STATISTICS

- Location: The Abbey Craig, Stirling
- Architect: J T Rochead
- Style: Scottish Baronial
- Foundation stone laid: 1863
- Construction completed: 1869
- Cost: £18,000
- Height: 220 feet
- Base measurement: 54 feet square
- Number of steps to top: 246
- Statues in the Hall of Heroes: Sir David Brewster, Robert the Bruce, George Buchanan, Robert Burns, Thomas Carlyle, Thomas Chalmers, William Ewart Gladstone, John Knox, David Livingstone, Hugh Miller, William Murdock, Allan Ramsay, Sir Walter Scott, Adam Smith, Robert Tannahill, James Watt

NELSON'S MONUMENT EDINBURGH – VITAL STATISTICS

- Location: Calton Hill, Edinburgh
- Reason for construction: Commemoration of Nelson's victory at the Battle of Trafalgar 1805
- Architect: Robert Burns
- Date of construction: 1816
- Design: Upturned telescope
- Height: 108 feet (approx 33.3 metres)
- Number of steps to top: 143
- On top of Nelson's monument is a time ball, which drops at one o'clock (p.m) every day. This was originally constructed to be visible from the port of Leith, enabling ships to set their chronometers.

I SWEAR
Did you know ... ?

The first printed use of the F-word was in the poetry of court poet William Dunbar (c.1460–c.1520) in 1503, in the poem *Ane Brash of Wowing* or *In Secreit Place*. Other early recorded uses of the word are from Scots writers which may indicate that the word was not taboo in Scotland at this time or that the Scots were just less inhibited about the vocabulary of their literature.

LOCATIONS OF HIGHLAND GAMES AROUND SCOTLAND

Aberdeen	Argyllshire
Abefeldy	Arisaig
Aberlour	Assynt
Abernethy	Atholl and Bredalbane
Aboyne	Ballater
Airth	Balloch
Alva	Balquhidder, Lochernhead and
Arbroath	Strathyre
Ardrossan	Barra

Bathgate and West Lothian

Bearsden

Beauly

Birnam

Blackford

Blair Atholl

Blairgowrie

The Border Gathering

Braemar

Bridge of Allan

Brodick

Burntisland

Bute

Caithness

Callander

Campbeltown

Carrick

Ceres (the oldest event)

Chirnside

Cornhill

Cowal and Dunoon

Cortachy

Crieff

Cupar

Dingwall

Dornoch

Drumtochty

Dufftown

Dunbeath

Dundonald

Dunrobin

Durness

Elgin

Forfar

Forres

Glenfinnan

Glengarry

Glenisla

Glenurquhart

Gourock

Grantown on Spey

Halkirk

Helmsdale

Inverary

Invercharron

Invergordon

Inverkeithing

Inverness

Kenmore

Killin

Kilmore and Kilbride

Lesmahagow

Lewis

Lochaber

Lochcarron

Lochearnhead

Loch Ness

Lonach

Luss

Mallaig and Morar

Markinch

Mey

Montrose

Morvern

Mull

Nairn

Newburgh

Newtonmore

North Berwick

North Uist

Oban

Oldmeldrum

Peebles

Penicuik

Perth

Pitlochry

Rosneath and Clynder

Shotts

Skye
Southend
South Uist
St Andrews
Stirling
Stonehaven
Strathallan
Strathardle

Strathconon
Strathmiglo
Strathpeffer
Tain
Taynuilt
Thornton
Tomintoul

HIGHLAND GAMES EVENTS

Traditionally, clan chiefs would organise contests to find the strongest men for bodyguards, the fastest men for couriers and the fittest men for their army The best pipers and dancers were hired as entertainers. Of course, these days the games are family events for entertainment only.

tossing the caber
tug o' war
throwing the weight/putting the shot
throwing the hammer
highland dancing
track and field events – running jumping pole vault

Some also include novelty items such as:
fly casting
children's events
hurling the haggis (a ladies' event)
pillow fight
strongest man
cycling
clay pigeon shooting

DISTILLERIES PRODUCING
NAMED SINGLE MALT WHISKIES

There are hundreds of distilleries around Scotland, particularly in the area around the Spey Valley. Some of them produce whisky for blends only, but others produce their own single malt. Quite often there are a number of different bottlings available.

Many of these distilleries have visitor centres and conduct regular tours for visitors. Others are willing to accommodate visitors by appointment. A few distilleries do not allow visitors. It is always worth telephoning to enquire first, in order to save yourself a wasted journey.

Most of the single malts are named after the distilleries where they are produced. In cases where the name of the malt does not correspond to the name of the distillery, the malt is also listed here:

Aberfeldy Distillery, Aberfeldy , Perthshire. Founded 1826.

Aberlour Distillery, Aberlour. Founded 1826.

Alt na Bhainne Distillery, near Dufftown, Speyside. Founded 1975.

An Cnoc Distillery, Huntly, Aberdeenshire. Founded 1893. Cnoc Single Malt.

Ardmore Distillery, Kennethmont, Aberdeenshire. Founded 1898.

Arran Distillery, Lochranza, Isle of Arran. Founded 1995.

Aultmore Distillery, Aultmore, Keith, Banffshire. Founded 1896.

Auchroisk Distillery, Mulben, Banffshire. Founded 1974. The Singleton.

Balblair Distillery, Balblair, Ross-shire. Founded 1790.

Balmenach Distillery, Cromdale, Morayshire. Founded 1824.

Balvenie Distillery, Dufftown, Banffshire. Founded 1892.

Ben Nevis Distillery, Fort William. Founded 1825.

Benriach Distillery, by Elgin. Founded 1898.

Benrinnes Distillery, Aberlour. Founded 1826.

Benromach Distillery, Forres, Morayshire. Founded 1898.

Bladnoch Distillery, Dumfries and Galloway. Founded 1817.

Blair Athol Distillery, Blair Athol, Perthshire. Founded 1798.

Bowmore Distillery, Bowmore, Islay. Founded 1779.

Bunnahabhain, Distillery, Port Askaig, Islay. Founded 1881.

Caol Ila Distillery, Port Askaig, Islay. Founded 1846.

Cardhu Distillery, Aberlour, Speyside. Founded 1824.

Clynelish Distillery, Brora, Sutherland. Founded 1819.

Cragganmore Distillery, Ballindalloch, Aberdeenshire. Founded 1896.

Craigellachie Distillery, Aberlour, Speyside. Founded 1891.

Dailuane Distillery, Carron, Morayshire. Founded 1851.

Dalwhinnie Distillery, Dalwhinnie, Perthshire. Founded 1897.

Deanston Distillery, Doune, Perthshire. Founded 1785.

Drumguish Distillery, Kingussie. Founded 1962.

Dufftown Distillery, Dufftown, Banffshire. Founded 1896.

Edradour Distillery, Pitlochry. Founded 1825.

Fettercairn Distillery, Laurencekirk, Kincardineshire. Founded 1824.

Glenburgie Distillery, by Alva, Forres. Founded 1810.

Glendronach Distillery, Forgue, Aberdeenshire. Founded 1826.

Macduff Distillery, Macduff, Banffshire. Founded 1962.

Glendullan Distillery, Dufftown, Keith, Banffshire. Founded 1896.

Glen Elgin Distillery, Elgin, Morayshire. Founded 1898.

Glenfarclas Distillery, Ballindalloch, Banffshire. Founded 1836.

Glenfiddich Distillery, Dufftown, Banffshire. Founded 1886.

Glen Garioch Distillery, Old Meldrum, Aberdeenshire. Founded 1797.

Glen Goyne Distillery, Drumgoyne, Stirlingshire. Founded 1833.

Glen Grant Distillery, Rothes, Banffshire. Founded 1840.

Glen Keith Distillery, Keith, Banffshire. Founded 1957.

Glenkinchie Distillery, Pencaitland, West Lothian. Founded 1837.

Glenlivet Distillery, Ballindalloch, Banffshire. Founded 1824.

Glenlossie Distillery, Elgin, Morayshire. Founded 1876.

Glenmorangie Distillery, Tain. Founded 1843.

Glen Moray Distillery, Elgin, Morayshire. Founded 1897.

Glen Ord Distillery, Muir of Ord, Ross-shire. Founded 1838.

Glenrothes Distillery, Rothes, Banffshire. Founded 1878.

Glen Scotia Distillery, Campbeltown. Founded 1832.

Glen Spey Distillery, Rothes, Aberlour, Banffshire. Founded 1870s.

Glen Turret Distillery, Crieff. Founded 1775.

Highland Park Distillery, Kirkwall, Orkney. Founded 1790.

Imperial Distillery, Carron, Banffshire. Founded 1897.

Inchgower Distillery, Buckie, Banffshire. Founded 1871.

Isle of Jura, Distillery, Jura. Founded 1810.

Knockando Distillery, Morayshire. Founded 1898.

Lagavulin Distillery, Port Ellen, Islay. Founded 1816.

Laphroaig Distillery, Port Ellen, Islay. Founded 1815.

Loch Lomond Distillery, Alexandria, Loch Lomondside. Founded 1965.
    Inchmurrin, Old Rosdhu.

Longmorn Distillery, Elgin, Morayshire. Founded 1894.

Macallan Distillery, Craigellachie. Founded 1824.

Mannochmore Distillery, Elgin, Morayshire. Founded 1971.

Miltonduff Distillery, Elgin, Morayshire. Founded 1824. Miltonduff and
    Mosstowie.

Mortlach Distillery, Dufftown, Keith, Banffshire. Founded 1823

Oban Distillery, Oban, Argyll. Founded 1794.

Pulteney Distillery, Wick. Founded 1826. Old Pulteney.

Royal Brackla Distillery, Cawdor, Nairn, Morayshire. Founded 1812.

Royal Lochnagar Distillery, Ballater. Founded 1826

Speyburn Distillery, Rothes, Banffshire. Founded 1897.
Springbank Distillery, Campbeltown. Founded 1828.
Strathisla Distillery, Keith, Banffshire. Founded 1786.
Talisker Distillery, Carbost, Isle of Skye. Founded 1830.
Tandhu Distillery, Knockando. Founded 1897.
Teaninich Distillery, Alness, Ross-shire. Founded 1817.
Tobermory Distillery, Tobermory, Isle of Mull. Founded 1798.
Tomatin Distillery, Inverness-shire, Founded 1897.
Tomintoul Distillery, Ballindalloch. Founded 1964.
Tormore Distillery, Grantown-on-Spey. Founded 1958.

SCOTS WORDS FOR BEING DRUNK

battered	miraculous
bevvied	paralettic
birlin'	pished
bleezin'	reekin'
blootered	reelin'
faur-on (far on)	rubber
fleein'	steamboats
fou	steamin'
guttered	stoatin'
hammered	stocious
jaiked/jaiked up	suitably refreshed
leathered	tanked

THE REAL MACKAY OR McCOY?

Did you know...?

The origins of this phrase, meaning 'the geuine article', seem to lie in an historical confusion over the identity of the Mackay clan chief. Whatever the case, it was adopted in the nineteenth century as an advertising slogan for Mackay's whisky. Later, it crops up in the writings of RL Stevenson. Around 1900, it entered American usage as 'the real McCoy'. Americans maintain that it all started with a boxer called Kid McCoy, or, even better, the famous (Canadian) prohibition bootlegger, Bill McCoy. Who can tell?

THE SCOTTISH COURTS

The Scottish Executive justice department, under the Minister for Justice, is responsible for the operation of the courts, via the Scottish Court Service.

District Courts

These are courts which deal with minor offences (traffic violations, breach of the peace, vandalism, etc.) They are run by local authorities, and presided over by justices of the peace. Justices of the peace have been trained for service and are assisted by clerks, qualified in the law. The maximum fine that can be imposed in a district court is £2,500. The maximum sentence of imprisonment is 60 days.

Sheriff Courts

There are forty-nine sheriff courts in Scotland, each of which belongs to one of six Scottish sheriffdoms. Each sheriffdom is in the charge of a Sheriff Principle with a team of sheriffs, some of whom are attached to particular courts, whilst others move between different courts within the sheriffdom.

The sheriff courts deal with both criminal and civil cases and also handle fatal accident inquiries.

Criminal cases fall into two categories:

1 Summary procedure: the sheriff sits without a jury and decides both verdict and sentence. Minor offences are dealt with by summary procedure, and the sheriff is limited in his sentencing powers – a maximum fine of £5,000 and a maximum sentence of 3 months.

2 Solemn procedure: the case is heard by a sheriff and a jury of fifteen members. The jury decides the verdict. The sheriff has greater powers of sentencing in solemn procedure cases, which are more serious than summary cases. He may also decide to remit the case to the High Court, if he thinks the severity of the case merits a heavier sentence than he can impose.

Very serious cases, such as murder, rape and treason cannot be dealt with by the sheriff courts and will automatically be heard in the High Court of Justiciary.

A wide variety of civil cases are dealt with by the sheriff courts, including debt and contract litigation, property and tenancy disputes and matters of family law such as divorce and child custody.

The High Court of the Justiciary

The High Court of the Justiciary is Scotland's supreme criminal court. It acts as both a trial court and the court of appeal for criminal cases.

High court criminal trials may take place in any of the major towns and cities in Scotland. The most serious criminal cases are dealt with by the High Court, and are tried by a judge and a jury of fifteen men and women. Criminal cases are brought to the court in the name of the Lord Advocate and either an advocate or an advocate depute (Crown Counsel) will lead the prosecution.

As an appeal court, the High Court sits only in Parliament House in Edinburgh. It is the final court of appeal – there can be no further appeal once a case has been considered by the High Court. At least three judges will sit to consider an appeal against a conviction. Two or more judges will sit to consider an appeal against sentencing.

The Court of Session

The Court of Session is the supreme civil court of Scotland. There are two divisions in the Court of Session:

1 The Outer House, which consists of nineteen judges. Most cases are heard by one judge, who may sit with a civil jury of fifteen men and women.

2 The Inner House, a court of appeal, formed of two divisions of four judges. Appeals – from the Outer House, the Sheriff Court and from certain other Scottish tribunals – are considered by at least three judges.

Court of the Lord Lyon

The Lord Lyon King of Arms has jurisdiction on all questions of heraldry and the right to bear Arms. The Court also administers the relevant public registers. Appeals are made to the Court of Session.

Scottish Land Court

Established in 1911, its purpose is to resolve disputes arising in connection with agricultural or other holdings, and crofts. There is a Divisional Court for the hearing of applications, and a Full Court. The right of appeal is to the Court of Session, on points of law only.

SHERIFFDOMS AND SHERIFF COURTS IN SCOTLAND

GLASGOW AND STRATHKELVIN
Glasgow Sheriff Court

GRAMPIAN, HIGHLANDS AND ISLANDS
Aberdeen Sheriff Court
Banff Sheriff Court

Dingwall Sheriff Court
Dornoch Sheriff Court
Elgin Sheriff Court
Fort William Sheriff Court
Inverness Sheriff Court
Kirkwall Sheriff Court
Lerwick Sheriff Court
Lochmaddy Sheriff Court
Peterhead Sheriff Court
Portree Sheriff Court
Stonehaven Sheriff Court
Stornoway Sheriff Court
Tain Sheriff Court
Wick Sheriff Court

LOTHIAN AND BORDERS

Duns Sheriff Court
Edinburgh Sheriff Court
Haddington Sheriff Court
Jedburgh Sheriff Court
Linlithgow Sheriff Court
Peebles Sheriff Court
Selkirk Sheriff Court

NORTH STRATHCLYDE

Campbeltown Sheriff Court
Dumbarton Sheriff Court
Dunoon Sheriff Court

Greenock Sheriff Court
Kilmarnock Sheriff Court
Oban Sheriff Court
Paisley Sheriff Court
Rothesay Sheriff Court

SOUTH STRATHCLYDE, DUMFRIES AND GALLOWAY

Airdrie Sheriff Court
Ayr Sheriff Court
Dumfries Sheriff Court
Hamilton Sheriff Court
Kirkcudbright Sheriff Court
Lanark Sheriff Court
Stranraer Sheriff Court

TAYSIDE, CENTRAL AND FIFE

Alloa Sheriff Court
Arbroath Sheriff Court
Cupar Sheriff Court
Dundee Sheriff Court
Dunfermline Sheriff Court
Falkirk Sheriff Court
Forfar Sheriff Court
Kirkcaldy Sheriff Court
Perth Sheriff Court
Stirling Sheriff Court

DISTRICT COURTS IN SCOTLAND

(Where the title of the court does not indicate the location, this has been added)

Aberdeen
Aberdeenshire at Banff
Aberdeenshire at Inverurie
Aberdeenshire at Peterhead
Aberdeenshire at Stonehaven
Angus – located in Forfar

Argyll and Bute – located in
   Kilmory, Lochgilphead
Ayr and Girvan – located in Ayr
Clackmannanshire – located in Alloa
Dumfries and Galloway at Annan
Dumfries and Galloway at Dumfries

Dumfries and Galloway at Kirkcudbright
Dumfries and Galloway at Lockerbie
Dumfries and Galloway at Stranraer
Dundee
East Ayrshire at Cumnock
East Ayrshire at Kilmarnock
East Dunbartonshire at Kirkintilloch
East Dunbartonshire at Milngavie
East Lothian – located in Haddington
East Renfrewshire at Giffnock
Edinburgh
Falkirk
Fife at Cupar
Fife at Dunfermline
Fife at Kirkcaldy
Glasgow
Highland (Dingwall)
Highland (Dornoch)
Highland (Fort William)
Highland (Inverness)
Highland (Kingussie)
Highland (Nairn)
Highland (Portree)
Highland (Tain)
Highland (Wick)

Inverclyde – located in Greenock
Midlothian – located in Penicuik
Moray – located in Elgin
North Ayrshire – located in Irvine
North Lanarkshire at Coatbridge
North Lanarkshire at Cumbernauld
North Lanarkshire at Motherwell
Perth and Kinross – located in Perth
Renfrewshire – located in Paisley
Scottish Borders Berwickshire Division – located in Duns
Scottish Borders Ettrick and Lauderdale Division – located in Galashiels
Scottish Borders Roxburgh Division – located in Jedburgh
Scottish Borders Tweeddale Division – located in Peebles
South Lanarkshire at East Kilbride
South Lanarkshire at Hamilton
South Lanarkshire at Lanark
South Lanarkshire at Rutherglen
Stirling
West Dunbartonshire – located in Dumbarton
Western Isles – located in Stornoway, Isle of Lewis
West Lothian – located in Livingston

UNIVERSITY MOTTOES

Aberdeen University	*Initium Sapientiae Timor Domini* (The fear of the Lord is the beginning of wisdom)
Dundee University	*Magnificat Anima Mea Dominum* (My soul doth magnify the Lord)
Glasgow University	*Via, Veritas, Vita* (The way, the truth and the life)
St Andrews University	*Aien Aristeuein* (Always strive to be the best)
Stirling University	Innovation and Excellence

ORIGINS OF A TONGUE TWISTER

Round and round the Radical Road,
The radical rascal ran;
How many r's are in that?
Tell me if you can.

In the early nineteenth century in Scotland, unemployment was rising and faith in the government was low. Working conditions in the newly industrialised towns and cities were very poor and the working classes did not have a voice. There was already a history of radicalism in Scotland. In the 1790's the government had used strong measures to suppress the movement and several Radical leaders had been arrested and deported to the colonies. The movement had subsided into relative inactivity during the Napoleonic wars, but now, with the war over, food prices rising rapidly and industrial unrest increasing, simmering discontent turned to outright revolt. Handloom weavers from Paisley, whose jobs were threatened by rapid industrialisation in the weaving industry, were at the centre of the unrest, which came to a head in April 1820. Marches were organised and there was a mass strike in factories in the west of central Scotland. Leaders of the movement were intercepted on a march towards Falkirk. Three were hung and many more were deported. The Radical rising had failed, but it found widespread sympathy throughout Scotland.

When it was proposed that a road should be built at the foot of Salisbury Crags on Arthur's Seat in Edinburgh, Sir Walter Scott put forward the idea that unemployed weavers from Paisley should be put to work on the project. The road is still in existence today and is called the Radical Road after the men who built it.

TRY OUT YOUR TYPING WITH BURNS

The plot of Tam o' Shanter summarised in two holoalphabetic sentences:

Tam, jesting, boozes quickly while vexed wife pouts wrathfully.
Tam gawps at devilish frenzy but jumping mare forces quick exit.

MORTON AND THE MAIDEN
Did you know ...?

The most common methods of execution in Scotland were hanging and beheading, but from the middle of the sixteenth century until the beginning of the eighteenth century, there was another alternative – the Maiden. The Maiden was a device which worked along the same principles as the guillotine which was to become so notorious in the French Revolution in 1789. A blade, suspended from the top of the Maiden's frame, was dropped onto the victim's neck, severing the head from the shoulders.

The Maiden was introduced to Scotland by James Douglas, the 4th Earl of Morton, who was Regent of Scotland in the early years of James VI's reign. Some say Morton invented it.

The Maiden had a number of prominent victims, including Archibald Campbell, 9th Earl of Argyll, who was beheaded after rebelling against King James VII in 1685. The most famous victim of the Maiden was Morton himself. He was found guilty of treason in 1580 and executed in 1581.

The saying 'he who invented the Maiden first hanselled it' is not quite true. Morton was not its inaugural victim. But we have to wonder what he was thinking as he was taken to face his fate – the irony of the situation can not have escaped him.

FACES ON NOTES

Portraits of the following people have featured on Scottish banknotes in the last thirty years:

Her Majesty Queen Elizabeth II	Commemorative banknote (£5) issued by the Royal Bank of Scotland to mark the Queen's Golden Jubilee. Issued February 6, 2002.
Her Majesty Queen Elizabeth the Queen Mother	Commemorative banknote (£5) issued by the Royal Bank of Scotland to mark

	the occasion of the Queen Mother's 100th birthday. Issued August 5, 2000.
Robert Louis Stevenson	Commemorative banknote issued by the Royal Bank of Scotland to mark the centenary of Stevenson's death. Issued December 3, 1994.
Alexander Graham Bell	Commemorative banknote issued by the Royal Bank of Scotland to mark the 150th anniversary of Bell's birth.
Lord Ilay	Lord Ilay, the Royal Bank of Scotland's first governor, has featured on standard issue Royal Bank of Scotland notes of all denominations since September 1987.
Sir Walter Scott	Scott features on the front of banknotes of all denominations issued by the Bank of Scotland.
Lord Kelvin	The portrait of Lord Kelvin features on current £100 notes issued by the Clydesdale Bank.
Adam Smith	Smith appears on the front of £50 notes issued by the Clydesdale Bank.
Robert the Bruce	A portrait of Bruce appears on the front of the Clydesdale Bank's current £20 note.
Mary Slessor	A portrait of Mary Slessor, the Scots missionary in Nigeria, appears on the Clydesdale Bank's current issue of £10 notes.
Robert Burns	Burns's portrait features on the front of the current issue of £5 notes by the Clydesdale Bank.
Alexander 'Greek' Thomson	This famous Glasgow architect's portrait appeared o a commemorative note issued by the Clydesdale bank to mark Glasgow's election as 'City of Architecture and Design' in 1999.

OPERATIONAL LIGHTHOUSES AROUND SCOTLAND

The Operating Authority for the lighthouses around Scotland is the Northern Lighthouse Board, formerly The Commissioners for the Northern Lighthouses.

There are no manned lighthouses any more. The last manned lighthouse was automated in 2000. The Northern Lighthouse Board is now in the process of changing over many of their lights to work with solar energy. In addition to the Scottish lighthouses listed below, the Northern Lighthouse Board is responsible for lighthouses on the Isle of Man: Calf of Man (est. 1818), Chicken Rock (est. 1875), Douglas Head (est. 1859), Langness, Maughold Head, Point of Ayre, Point of Ayre (Winkie) and Thousla Rock.

Ailsa Craig 1886
Ardmore Point 1958
Ardnamurchan Lighthouse 1849
Ardrossan Lighthouse
Ardtornish 1927
Ardtreck 1904
Arnish Point 1853
Auskerry, Orkney 1866
Bagi Stack 1976
Balta Sound 1895
Barns Ness 1901
Barra Head 1833
Barrel of Butter 1980
Bass Rock 1902
Bell Rock 1811
Bressay 1858
Brother Isle 1978
Brough of Birsay 1925
Buchan Ness 1827
Bunessan 1901
Butt of Lewis 1862
Cailleach Head
Cairns of Coll 1909
Cairnbulg Briggs 1858
Calf of Eday 1909
Calvay 1891

Canna 1907
Cantick Head 1858
Cape Wrath 1828
Carloway 1892
Carragh An T'Striuth 1960
Carragh Mhor 1928
Cava 1898
Channel Rock, Castlebay
Chanonry 1846
Clythness 1916
Copinsay 1915
Corran
Corran Narrows North East 1860
Corsewall 1817
Covesea Skerries 1846
Craigton Point 1904
Crammag Head 1913
Cromarty 1846
Crowlin 1892
Davaar 1854
Duart Point 1901
Dubh Artach 1872
Dubh Sgeir, Castlebay
Dubh Sgeir, Kerrara
Dubh Sgeir, Luing
Duncansby Head 1924

Dunnet Head 1831

Dunollie 1892

Dunvegan

Eigg 1985

Eight Metre Rock

Eilean a Chuirn 1907

Eilean Glas 1789

Eilean Nan Gabhar 1968

Eilean Trodday 1908

Eileanan Dubha

Elie Ness 1908

Esha Ness 1929

Eyre Point 1938

Fair Isle South 1892

Fair Isle North 1892

Fidra 1885

Fife Ness 1975

Firths Voe 1909

Fladda 1860

Flannan Islands 1899

Foula 1986

Fugla Ness 1893

Gamhna Gigha

Gasey Island 1985

Gasker

Girdle Ness 1833 1833

Green Island 1906

Grey Rocks 1890

Gruney 1976

Haskeir

Helliar Holm 1893

Hestan Island 1850

Hillswick 1895

Holborn Head 1862

Holm of Skaw 1895

Holy Island Inner 1906

Holy Island Outer 1906

Hoo Stack 1986

Hoxa Head 1901

Hoy Sound High 1851

Hoy Sound Low 1851

Hyskeir 1904

Inchcolm, Forth Ports PLC 1858

Inchkeith 1804

Isle of May 1636, 1816

Killantringan 1900

Kinnaird Head 1787

Kylerhea 1892

Lady Isle 1903

Lady Rock 1907

Lismore 1833

Little Holm 1976

Little Ross 1843

Loch Eriboll 1894

Loch Indall 1869

Loch Ryan 1847

Longman Point

Lowther Rock 1910

Lunna Holm 1985

McArthur's Head 1861

Milaid Point 1912

Monach Isles 1867

Mousa 1951

Muckle Flugga 1854

Muckle Holm 1976

Muckle Roe 1897

Muckle Skerry

Mull of Eswick 1904

Mull of Galloway 1830

Mull of Kintyre 1788

Na Cuiltean 1911

Neist Point 1909

Ness of Sound 1907

North Rona 1984

North Ronaldsay 1790

North Spit of Kerrara 1948

Noss Head 1849

Noup Head 1898

Oban NLB Pier
Ornsay 1857
Ornsay Beacon 1908
Out Skerries Whalsay 1854
Outer Skerry 1908
Oxcars, Forth Ports PLC 1886
Papa Stronsay 1907
Pentland Skerries 1794
Pladda 1790
Point of Fethaland 1977
Port Ellen 1832
Rattray Head 1895
Reisa An T'Struith 1892
Rhinns of Islay 1825
Rona 1857
Roseness 1905
Rova Head
Ruadh Sgeir 1906
Rubh Glas Front, Vatersay 1958
Rubh Glas Rear, Vatersay 1956
Rubh Re
Rubh Uisenish 1938
Rubh'A'Chruidh
Rubha Cadail 1952
Rubha Nan Gall 1857
Ruff Reef 1909
Rumble Rock
Ruvaal 1859
Sanda 1858
Sandaig 1910
Scalasaig 1903
Scarinish 1897

Scurdie Ness 1870
Sgeir Bhuidhe 1903
Sgeir Leadh, Castlebay 1891
Sgeir-Na-Cailleach 1958
Skate of Marrister 1986
Skerry of Ness 1981
Skerryvore 1844
Skervuile 1865
Sleat Point
St Abbs Head 1862
Start Point 1806
Stroma 1896
Stromness NLB Pier
Sule Skerry 1895
Sumburgh Head 1821
Suther Ness 1904
Swona 1906
Symbister Ness 1904
Tarbat Ness 1830
The Garvellachs 1904
Tiumpan Head 1900
Tod Head 1897
Tor Ness 1937
Turnberry 1873
Ushenish 1857
Uyeasound 1946
Vaila Sound 1894
Vaternish 1924
Ve Skerries 1979
Weaver Point 1891
Whitehill 1904

FICTIONAL WORKS OF SIR WALTER SCOTT

Waverley, 1814
Guy Mannering, 1815
The Antiquary, 1816
The Black Dwarf (Tales of My Landlord, First Series), 1816

A Tale of Old Mortality (Tales of My Landlord, First Series), 1816
Rob Roy, 1817
The Heart of Midlothian
(Tales of My Landlord, Second Series), 1816
The Bride of Lammermoor
(Tales of My Landlord, Third Series), 1819
A Legend of Montrose
(Tales of My Landlord, Third Series), 1819
Ivanhoe,1819
The Monastery (Tales From Benedictine Sources), 1820
The Abbot (Tales From Benedictine Sources), 1820
Kenilworth, 1821
The Pirate, 1821
The Fortunes of Nigel, 1822
Peveril of the Peak, 1823
Quentin Durward, 1823
St Ronan's Well, 1823
Redgauntlet, 1824
The Betrothed (Tales of the Crusaders), 1825
The Talisman (Tales of the Crusaders), 1825
Woodstock, 1826
Chronicles of the Canongate, First Series, 1827
The Fair Maid of Perth (Chronicles of the Canongate, Second Series), 1828
Anne of Geierstein, 1829
Count Robert of Paris (Tales of My Landlord, Fourth Series), 1831
Castle Dangerous (Tales of My Landlord, Fourth Series), 1831

POETICAL WORKS OF SIR WALTER SCOTT

Minstrelsy of the Scottish Border, 1802–3
The Lay of the Last Minstrel, 1805
Marmion, 1807
The Lady of the Lake, 1810
The Vision of Don Roderick, 1811
Rokeby, 1813
The Bridal of Triermain, 1813
The Lord of the Isles, 1815
The Field of Waterloo, 1815
Harold the Dauntless, 1817

THE SCOTTISH MUNROS

In 1891, Sir Hugh Munro first published the Munro tables, which named 280 peaks in Scotland above the height of 3000 feet. The list of Munros has been revised over the years and the most recent revision was in 1997. There are now 284 peaks recognised as true Munros. The following list shows them in ascending order, giving the height of each peak to the nearest metre.

Ben Vane 915m	Bla Bheinn 928m
Sgurr nan Ceannaichean 915m	Mayar 928m
Beinn Teallach 915m	Meall nan Eun 928m
Beinn a'Chlaidheimh 916m	Moruisg 928m
Beinn a'Cleibh 916m	A'Chailleach (Monadh Liath) ..930m
Carn Aosda 917m	Beinn Bhreac 931m
Gealcharn 917m	Ben Chonzie 931m
Sgurr a'Mhadaidh (SW peak) .918m	Meall Buidhe (Glen Lyon) 932m
A' Ghlas-bheinn 918m	Beinn Chabhair 933m
Creag nan Damh 918m	Fionn Bheinn 933m
Meall na Teanga 918m	Maol Chean-Dearg 933m
Ruadh Stac Mhor 918m	The Cairnwell 933m
Gairich 919m	Am Basteir 934m
Cairn Sgulain 920m	Meall a'Chrasgaidh 934m
An Socach (Glen Affric) 921m	A'Bhuidheanach Bheag 936m
Sgiath Chuil 921m	Beinn na Lap 937m
Beinn Alligin – Tom na Gruagaich	Beinn Sgulaird 937m
....922m	Beinn Tarsuin 937m
An Coileachan 923m	Sron a'Choire Ghairbh 937m
Sgurr nan Each 923m	Luinne Bheinn 939m
Sgurr nan Eag 924m	Mount Keen 939m
Creag Pitridh 924m	Mullach nan Coirean 939m
Buchaille Etive Beag -Stob Coire	Beinn a'Chroin 940m
Raineach 925m	Carn na Chaim 941m
Beinn Liath Mhor 926m	Carn Dearg (Loch Ossian) 941m
Beinn Narnain 926m	Binnein Beag 943m
Geal Charn 926m	Ben Vorlich (Loch Lomond) 943m
Meall a'Choire Leith 926m	An Socach (Glen Ey) West Summit .
Seana Braigh 926m	....944m
Ben Hope 927m	Sgurr Dubh Mhor 944m
Eididh nan Clach Geala 927m	Bidean a'Choire Sheasgaich 945m

Carn Dearg (Monadh Liath) ...945m
Sgurr na Sgine 945m
Stob a'Choire Odhair 945m
Carn Bhac 946m
Meall Buidhe (Knoydart) 946m
Beinn Tulaichean 946m
Creag a'Mhaim 947m
Driesh 947m
Beinn Buidhe 948m
Sgurr Mhic Choinnich 948m
Meall Gorm 949m
Meall Chuaich 951m
Beinn Mhanach 953m
Meall Dearg 953m
Sgurr nan Coireachan (Glen Dessary)
....953m
Am Faichagach 954m
Beinn Liath Mhor Fannaich 954m
Stob Gaibhre 955m
Buachaille Etive Mor – Stob na
  Broige 956m
Saileag 956m
Sgurr nan Coireachan (Glen Finnan)
  956m
Carn Ghluasaid 957m
Tom Buidhe 957m
Bruach na Frithe 958m
Buachaille Etive Beag – Stob Dubh
  (Glencoe) 958m
Tolmount 958m
Beinn Fhionnlaidh (Appin) 959m
Meall Glas 959m
Beinn nan Aighenan 960m
Stuchd an Lochain 960m
Ben Klibreck – Meall nan Cor 961m
Sgorr Ruadh 962m
Carn a'Chlamain 963m
Sgurr nan Gillean 963m
Sgurr Thuilm 963m

Sgurr nan Gillean 964m
Sgurr nan Banachdich – North Peak
....965m
Ben More (Mull) 966m
Aonach Eagach – Sgor nam
  Flannaidh 967m
A'Mhaighdean 967m
Meall Garbh (Glen Lyon) 968m
Sgurr a'Ghreadaidh 973m
Ben Lomond 974m
Beinn Sgritheall 974m
A'Mharconaich 975m
Carn a'Gheoidh 975m
Carn Liath (Beinn a'Ghlo) 975m
Stuc a'Chroin 975m
Meall nan Ceapraichean 977m
Stob Ban (Grey Corries) 977m
Beinn Dubhchraig 978m
Ciste Dhubh 979m
Stob Coire Sgriodain 979m
Beinn a'Chochuill 980m
Cona Mheall 980m
Creag Mhor (Glen Lyon) 981m
Maol Chinn-dearg 981m
Slioch 981m
An Gearanach 982m
Mullach na Dheiragain 982m
Ben Vorlich (Loch Earn) 985m
Beinn Alligin – Sgurr Mhor ...986m
Lurg Mhor 986m
Sgurr Deag, The Inaccessible
  Pinnacle 986m
Conival 987m
Creag Leacach 987m
Druim Shionnach 987m
Gaor Bheinn (Gulvain) 987m
Beinn Eunaich 989m
Sgurr Ban (Letterewe) 989m
Sgairneach Mhor 991m

Carn nan Gobhar (Glen Cannich) ...
....992m

Carn nan Gobhar (Glen Strathfarrar)
....992m

Sgurr Alasdair 992m

Beinn Eighe – Spidean Coire nan
Clach 993m

Sgurr na Ruaidhe 993m

Carn an Fhidhieir (Carn Ealar) ....
....994m

Sgor na h-Ulaidh 994m

An Caisteal 995m

Spidean Mialach 996m

A'Chailleach (Fannichs) 997m

Glas Bheinn Mhor 997m

Ben More Assynt 998m

Broad Cairn 998m

Stob Diamh 998m

Sgurr Breac 999m

Sgurr Choinnich 999m

Stob Ban (Mamores) 999m

Aonach Meadhoin 1001m

Beinn a'Bheithir – Sgor Dhonuill ....
....1001m

Meall Greigh 1001m

Sail Chaorainn 1002m

Sgurr na Carnach 1002m

Sgurr Mor (Loch Quoich) 1003m

Beinn an Dothaidh 1004m

Sgurr an Lochain 1004m

The Devil's Point 1004m

Beinn Fhionnlaidh (Glen Cannich) ..
....1005m

An Sgarsoch 1006m

Carn Liath (Loch Laggan) 1006m

Maoile Lunndaidh 1007m

Beinn Dearg (Atholl) 1008m

Beinn Eighe – Ruadh-stac Mor ....
....1010m

Sgurr an Doire Leathain 1010m

Sgurr Eilde Mor 1010m

The Saddle 1010m

Beinn Ime 1011m

Beinn Udlamain 1011m

Cairn Bannoch 1012m

Garbh Chioch Mhor 1013m

Beinn Bheoil 1019m

Carn an Tuirc 1019m

Mullach Clach a'Bhlair 1019m

Mullach Coire Mhic Fhearchair ....
....1019m

Ladhar Bheinn 1020m

Aonach air Chrith 1021m

Buachaille Etive Mor – Stob Dearg
(Glencoe) 1022m

Liathach – Mullach an Rathain ....
....1023m

Beinn a'Bheithir – Sgorr Dhearg .....
....1024m

Ben Challum 1025m

Sgurr a'Mhaorich 1027m

Sgurr na Ciste Duibhe 1027m

Carn Gorm 1028m

Ben Oss 1029m

Carn an Righ 1029m

Am Bodach 1032m

Beinn Fhada 1032m

Carn Dearg (Loch Pattack) ...1034m

Gleouraich 1035m

Sgurr a'Bhealaich Dherg 1036m

Carn a'Mhaim 1037m

Beinn Achaladair 1038m

Meall Ghaordaidh 1039m

Sgurr na Ciche 1040m

Carn Mairg 1042m

Meall nan Tarmachan 1044m

Stob Coir'an Albannaich 1044m

Beinn Iutharn Mhor 1045m

Ben Wyvis – Glas Leathad Mhor 1046m
Chno Dearg 1046m
Cruach Ardrain 1046m
Carn an t-Sagairt Mor 1047m
Creag Mhor (Glen Lochay) ... 1047m
Geal Charn (Loch Laggan) ... 1049m
Sgurr Fhuar-thuill 1049m
Beinn a'Chaorainn 1050m
Glas Tulaichean 1051m
Sgurr a'Chaorachain 1053m
Stob Poite Coire Ardair 1053m
Toll Creagach 1054m
Liathach – Spidean a'Choire Leith 1055m
Na Gruagaichean 1056m
An Teallach – Sgurr Fiona 1060m
An Teallach – Bidein a'Ghlas Thuill 1062m
Cairn of Claise 1064m
Sgurr Fhuaran 1067m
Glas Maol 1068m
An Socach (Glen Cannich) 1069m
Meall Corranaich 1069m
Braigh Coire Chruinn-bhalgain . 1070m
Stob Coire Sgreamhach 1072m
Beinn Dorain 1076m
Beinn Heasgarnich 1078m
Ben Starav 1078m
Beinn a'Chreachain 1081m
Beinn a'Chaorainn (Cairngorms) 1082m
Schiehallion 1083m
Sgurr a'Choire Ghlais 1083m
Beinn Dearg (Ross-shire) 1084m
Beinn a'Chlachair 1087m
Bynack More 1090m
Stob Ghabhar 1090m
Sgurr nan Clach Geala 1093m

Sgurr Choinnich Mor 1094m
Sgurr a'Mhaim 1099m
Creise 1100m
Beinn Eibhinn 1102m
Mullach Fraoch-choire 1102m
Beinn Ghlas 1103m
Stob a'Choire Mheadhoin 1105m
Meall a'Bhuiridh 1108m
Sgurr nan Conbhairean 1109m
Sgurr Mor (Fannichs) 1110m
White Mounth – Carn a'Coire Bhaideach 1110m
Tom a'Choinich 1112m
Monadh Mor 1113m
Stob Coire Easain 1115m
Aonach Beag (Badenoch) 1116m
Stob Coire an Laoigh 1116m
An Stuc 1118m
Meall Garbh (Lawers) 1118m
Stob Gaoith 1118m
A'Chralaig 1120m
Beinn a'Ghlo – Carn nan Gabhar 1120m
Ben Cruachan 1126m
An Riabhachan 1129m
Ben Lui 1130m
Binnein Mor 1130m
Creag Meagaidh 1130m
Geal-Charn (Loch Pattack) ... 1132m
Ben Alder 1148m
Bidean nam Bian 1150m
Sgurr na Lapaich 1150m
Sgurr nan Ceathreamhnan ... 1151m
Derry Cairngorm 1155m
Lochnagar – Cac Carn Beag . 1155m
Beinn Bhrotain 1157m
Stob Binnein 1165m
Ben Avon – Leabaidh an Daimh Bhuidhe 1171m

Ben More (Crianlarich) 1174m	Aonach Mor 1221m
Stob Choire Claurigh 1177m	Aonach Beag (Lochaber) 1234m
Mam Sodhail 1181m	Cairn Gorm 1245m
Beinn Mheadhoin 1182m	Sgor an Lochain Uaine 1258m
Carn Eige 1183m	Cairn Toul 1291m
Beinn a'Bhuird – North Top 1197m	Braeriach 1296m
Ben Lawers 1214m	Ben Macdui 1309m
Carn Mor Dearg 1220m	Ben Nevis 1344m

BRAVE IMPOSTER
Did you know ... ?

After the Battle of Culloden, Bonnie Prince Charlie spent many weeks on the run, hiding in remote shelters in various parts of the west of Scotland. Wherever he went, soldiers of the Hanoverian army were never far behind. One of the places where the prince took refuge was in Glenmoriston.

Roderick Mackenzie was a merchant from Edinburgh. He was travelling through Glenmoriston in the summer of 1746 when he encountered a group of redcoats who were hunting for Bonnie Prince Charlie. Mackenzie bore an uncanny resemblance to the prince. The redcoats thought that they had indeed found the royal fugitive and when Roderick Mackenzie did not co-operate with their questioning, they shot him. Rather than trying to persuade the redcoats of his real identity, Mackenzie called out in his dying moments: 'Alas, you have killed your prince!' His killers cut off his head and carried it to Fort Augustus, believing that this was the proof that Bonnie Prince Charlie was dead.

In Glenmoriston at least, the prince was safer than he had ever been, thanks to one man's bravery. A cairn has been erected in Glenmoriston in honour of Roderick Mackenzie.

INVENTORS

James Anderson (1739–1808)	Inventor of a small plough to be drawn by two horses.
Neil Arnott (1788–1874)	Invented a smokeless, economical stove. Designed a water–bed for invalids.
Alexander Bain (1810–77)	Invented the first electromagnetic clock. Was the first to transmit time signals telegraphically. Designed a fax machine.
John Logie Baird (1888–1946)	First to demonstrate television.
Robert Blair (1748–1828)	Invented the aplanatic telescope.
Alexander Graham Bell (1847–1922)	Inventor of the telephone.
Patrick Bell (1799–1869)	Inventor of a mechanised reaper
David Brewster (1781–1868)	Invented the kalaedoscope (1816). Designed a polyzonal lens for use in lighthouse lights.
Henry Brougham (1778–1868)	Designed the horse-drawn carriage of the same name.
David Dunbar Buick (1854–1929)	Devised a method for bonding enamel to iron, which was used in the manufacture of baths.
James Chalmers (1782–1853)	Invented the adhesive postage stamp (1834).
Dugald Clerk (1854–1932)	Invented a two-stroke gas engine which could also be used with petrol (1881).
Robert Davidson (1804–94)	Invented and tested a battery-powered electric locomotive.
James Dewar (1842–1923)	Invented the vacuum flask. Also discovered the process for producing liquid hydrogen.
Thomas Drummond (1797–1840)	Developed limelight. Invented the Drummond Light, used in lighthouses.
John Boyd Dunlop (1840–1921)	Developed a pneumatic tyre for commercial production (See also Robert William Thomson)

Sir Keith Elphinstone (1864–1944)	Designed a speedometer for cars.
William Fairbairn (1789–1874)	Invented a machine for riveting boilers. Built the first wrought –iron boat (1830). Developed rectangular wrought iron tubes for bridge construction – most notably, the Menai Bridge.
Patrick Ferguson (1744–1780)	Invented a breech-loading rifle (1776).
Alexander John Forsyth (1769–1843)	Invented the percussion cap.
William Brownie Garden (1869–1960)	Invented the revolving blackboard.
William Ged (1690–1749)	Invented stereotyping.
James Gregory (1638–75)	Invented the Gregorian telescope (1661) and did pioneering work in calculus.
Sir Isaac Holden (1807–97)	Invented the lucifer match.
Sir John Leslie (1766–1832)	Invented a hygrometer, a differential thermometer, the pyroscope, atmometer and aethrioscope.
John Loudon MacAdam (1756–1836)	Invented a process of constructing roads from compacted stones and gravel – Macadamisation.
Charles Macintosh (1766–1843)	Invented and produced the first waterproof cloth (1823).
Kirkpatrick Macmillan (1813–78)	Inventor of the bicycle (1840).
William McNaught (1813–81)	Invented the compound steam engine.
Andrew Meikle (1719–1811)	Invented a drum threshing machine.
Patrick Miller (1730–1815)	Invented the paddle wheel and used it to test the first steam ship on Dalswinton Loch (1788).
Alexander Muirhead (1848–1920)	Invented duplexing (simultaneous telegraph messages in both directions) (1875).
William Murdock (1754–1839)	Invented a high-pressure steam engine on wheels. (1792).
John Napier (1550–1617)	Invented a calculating machine, called 'Napier's Bones'. Invented logarithms.

James Nasmyth (1808–90)	Invented the steam hammer (1839).
James Paterson (1770–1840)	Invented a process for the manufacture of fishing nets.
Robert Stirling (1790–1878)	Invented the Stirling external combustion hot-air engine (1816).
Alan Archibald Campbell Swinton (1863–1930)	Pioneered X-ray photography for medical purposes.
William Symington (1763–1831)	Patented an engine for powering steamboats. Constructed the *Charlotte Dundas*, the first practical steamship ever built, in 1802.
Charles Tennant (1768–1838)	Invented solid bleaching powder with Charles Macintosh.
Robert William Thomson (1822–73)	Invented the pneumatic rubber tyre, which was later developed by Dunlop.
William Wallace (1768–1843)	Invented the Eidograph.
Robert Watson-Watt (1892–1973)	Invented radar.
James Watt (1736–1819)	Invented the first practical steam engine.
Robert Wilson (1803–82)	Invented the double action screw propeller (later to be used in torpedoes).
James Young (1811–33)	Invented the process of distilling paraffin oil from shale.

MEDICAL PIONEERS

James Braid (1795–1860)	Trained as a surgeon. Became involved in pioneering work in hypnotism, particularly in the treatment of nervous disorders.
William Cullen (1710–90)	Author of First Lines of the Practice of Physic (1778–9). First chair in medicine at Glasgow Medical School.
Ian Donald (1910–87)	Pioneered diagnostic ultrasound in pregnancy.
Sir Alexander Fleming (1881–1955)	Discovered penicillin (1928)
John Hunter (1728–93)	Carried out pioneering work in

	physiology, comparative anatomy, pathology and scientific surgery.
William Hunter (1718–83)	Carried out pioneering work in anatomy, obstetrics and midwifery.
James Lind (1716–94)	A physician with the Royal Navy who researched the cause and treatment of scurvy.
Ephraim MacDowell (1771–1830)	Performed the world's first ovariotomy (in America).
Sir William MacEwen (1848–1924)	Pioneered surgical techniques for operating on patients with brain tumours or trauma.
John James Rickard Macleod (1876–1935)	Carried out extensive studies on carbohydrate metabolism. Working with Frederick Banting, he discovered insulin and its function in lowering blood sugar in the body.
Patrick Manson (1844–1912)	Demonstrated that the mosquito carried malaria.
Sir James Young Simpson (1811–70)	Pioneered use of ether as an anaesthetic in childbirth. Researched and pioneered the use of chloroform for the same purpose (1847).
Marie Charlotte Carmichael Stopes (1880–1958)	Pioneered education on sex and contraception. Opened the first birth control clinic in Great Britain, in London (1921).

LEADERS IN SCIENCE, TECHNOLOGY AND ENGINEERING

Sir William Arrol (1839–1913)	Engineer. Constructed the second Tay Railway Bridge and the Forth Railway Bridge
Joseph Black (1728–1799)	Discovered the existence of gases other than air. Evolved the theory of latent heat.
James Bowman Lindsay (1799–1862)	Demonstrated constant electric light.

Robert Brown (1773–1858)	Observed the movement of particles in liquid ('Brownian movement'). Researched plant reproduction and cells.
Alexander Buchan (1828–1907)	Observed a pattern of hot and cold spells at fixed times of the year ('Buchan Spells')
Sir Sandford Fleming (1827–1915)	Emigrated to Canada where he became chief engineer of the Canadian Pacific Railway. Devised the international system of time zones.
Williamina Paton Fleming (1857–1911)	Emigrated to the US where she excelled as an astronomer. Discovered 10 of the 24 stellae novae recorded before 1911.
Thomas Graham (1805–1869)	Outstanding chemist who carried out extensive research on the properties of gases.
James Hall (1761–1832)	Eminent geologist and pioneer in the field of geochemistry.
Thomas Henderson (1798–1844)	First Astronomer Royal for Scotland.
James Hutton (1726–97)	Developed groundbreaking theories about how the Earth was formed that laid the foundations of the modern science of geology.
James Clerk Maxwell (1831–79)	Investigated colour perception. Demonstrated colour photography. Proved that light is made up of electromagnetic waves.
William Murdock (1754–1840)	Pioneered coal gas lighting.
Thomas Telford (1757–1834)	Engineer and surveyor who was responsible for the building of many bridges and oversaw several major construction programmes around Britain, including the Caledonian Canal (completed 1823), the Menai Suspension Bridge (completed 1826) and St Katherine's Docks in London (completed 1828)

Sir Robert McAlpine (1847–1934)   'Concrete Bob' pioneered the use of concrete in construction work in Scotland.

EARLY LUNATIC ASYLUMS IN SCOTLAND

Up until the late eighteenth century, the only accommodation provided for the mentally ill in Scotland's towns was in the local tollbooth (jail) or in the poorhouse. Conditions were invariably harsh and inhumane. In the eighteenth century, humanitarians began to put pressure on civic bodies to find funding for public buildings where mentally ill people would find a safe and calm retreat. The first purpose-built asylums in Scotland were as follows:

- The Royal Asylum, Infirmary and Dispensary, Montrose, founded 1782
- The Aberdeen Royal Lunatic Asylum, founded 1800
- The Royal Edinburgh Asylum, founded 1813
- The Glasgow Royal Asylum, founded 1814.
- The Dundee Royal Lunatic Asylum, founded 1820.
- The Murray Royal Lunatic Asylum, Perth, founded 1827.
- The Crichton Royal Lunatic Asylum, Dumfries, founded 1838.

SCOTTISH AIRPORTS AND AIRSTRIPS WHERE COMMERCIAL FLIGHTS LAND

Airports

Aberdeen
Barra
Benbecula
Campbeltown
Dundee
Edinburgh
Glasgow
Glengedale, Islay
Inverness (Dalcross)
Kirkwall, Orkney
Prestwick
Stornoway, Isle of Lewis
Sumburgh Airport, Shetland
Tiree
Wick

Airstrips

Shetland Isles: Fair Isle, Fetlar, Foula, Out Skerries, Papa Stour, Scatsta, Tingwall, Unst, Whalsay.

Orkney Isles: Eday, Flotta, North Ronaldsay, Papa Westray, Sanday, Stronsay, Westray

The shortest scheduled flight in the world is between the islands of Westray and Papa Westray. The flight lasts approximately two minutes.

TRADITIONAL FESTIVITIES

January 1	Ne'er Day.
–	Flambeaux Procession, Comrie, Perthshire.
–	Stonehaven Fireball Procession, Stonehaven, Aberdeenshire.
–	Orkney Ba' Game, Kirkwall.
–	Biggar's Bonfire, Biggar, Lanarkshire.

THE COMRIE FLAMBEAUX, PERTHSHIRE

Every New Year, on the stroke of midnight, the flambeaux are lit in Comrie. Tall, flaming torches made from branches are carried shoulder-high round the four compass points of the village in a parade of locals in fancy dress accompanied by a pipe band.

The wood for the flambeaux is cut in autumn. The torch end is wrapped in hessian and soaked in paraffin for several weeks. The flambeaux make a spectacular sight as they move around the village in the first moments of the New Year. They are kept alight while the winners of the fancy dress competition are announced, then they are extinguished in the River Earn. The ceremony is thought to have originated as a ritual for banishing evil spirits.

HOGMANAY FIREBALLS, STONEHAVEN, JANUARY 1

In days gone by, there were numerous places where Hogmanay was celebrated with the spectacle of fireballs. Stonehaven in the north east of Scotland now stands alone in upholding the fireball tradition. On New Year's Eve every year, just on the stroke of midnight, sixty local men take to the streets swinging flaming balls attached to ropes almost six feet long. Each fireball consists of an assortment of flammable material encased in wire mesh and weighs around twenty pounds – it takes quite a lot of strength to keep them swinging. A pipe band accompanies the processors as they parade through the town. The fireballs are swung all the way down to the harbour, where they are hurled into the sea.

ORKNEY BA' GAME, KIRKWALL

The Orkney Ba' Game in its present form has been played on Christmas Eve and Hogmanay every year since the mid-19th century. Two games are played – a men's game and a boys' game (for under-sixteens). The game is played between the 'Uppies', from 'up the gates', and the Doonies, from 'doon the gates' ('Gates' comes from the old Norse word *gata*, meaning 'road'). The boys' game is played during the morning – the men's game begins at 1.30 pm. The game begins when the ball – which is hand-made from leather, filled with cork – is thrown up in the air close to St Magnus Cathedral in Kirkwall. As many as 200 men take part, and the game, a spectacular but congenial scrum, can go on for several hours before either side reaches their goal and a winner is declared. The Uppies must get the ball to the top of the town in order to secure a win. The Doonies have the harbour as their goal. There was once a women's game too – once, and once only, in 1945!

January 2	Handsel Monday.
January 6	Uphaliday, the celebration of epiphany.
January 11	Burning the Clavie, Burghead, Morayshire.

THE BURNING OF THE CLAVIE, BURGHEAD

The Burning of the Clavie takes place on January 11 (officially recognised as Hogmany before 1660). Each year on the appointed date in Burghead, Moray, a half barrel filled with wood shavings and tar is nailed to a wooden post, ready to be set ablaze at the house of the provost and carried through the streets. The Clavie is set alight by a burning peat and a number of elected men – usually ten – take it in turns to hold it aloft as they make their way around the town. The first man to carry the Clavie after it has been set alight is the one who has been chosen to be Clavie King. Burning pieces of the Clavie – either picked up or given as gifts – are supposed to bring good luck in the coming year. The Clavie is carried to the site of an ancient fort on Doorie Hill and used as the foundation for a great bonfire. Those who manage to carry away a flaming ember from the fire to light a fire in their own hearth are considered fortunate.

January 12	Old New Years' Day.
January 25	Burns Night.
January, Last Tuesday	Up Helly Aa, Lerwick.

UP-HELLY-AA, SHETLAND

In the darkest months of winter, Shetlanders celebrate their Norse roots with a spectacular fire festival that is guaranteed to banish all signs of seasonal affective disorder. A parade of elected men, dressed as Vikings and led by a Jarl, take to the streets of Lerwick bearing flaming torches. They carry a full-scale replica of a Viking longboat with them. The procession is followed by hundreds of people, all of them dressed up and hundreds of them also bearing torches. The ceremony comes to a spectacular end when the Viking ship is set alight. The celebrations continue far into the night (or the next day) at private parties in various venues around the town.

February 2	Candlemas Day, a day for handfasting and betrothal.
February 14	Valentine's Day, celebrated all over the world, but Glasgow is said to be the site of the bones of St Valentine. Well, one of the sites. Supposedly.
End February	Gyro Night, Papa Westray, Orkney, last celebrated 1914, Boys with torches of fire would seek out the 'gygr' or troll woman and burn an effigy to chase out the winter.
Tuesday before Lent	Fastern's E'en, or Shrove Tuesday.
—	Jethart Ba', Jedburgh, Borders.
—	Denholm Ba' Day, Denholm village, Borders.
—	Beef Brose Night.
—	Bannock Night.
March 1	Whuppity Scourie, Lanark. At the ringing of a bell the local children run round the church of St Nicholas making as much noise as possible to chase away evil spirits.
April	Links Market, Kirkcaldy.
—	Kate Kennedy procession, St Andrews.

April 1	Huntigowk, hunting the gowk (fool), Scotland's April Fools' Day.
April 2	Tallie Day or Preen-tail day, Kirkcaldy, and Kirkwall, the April fool japes continue as tails are pinned on unsuspecting victims.
April 30	Beltane Fire Festival, Calton Hill, Edinburgh.
May 1	Beltane, May Day, pagan celebration of the height of spring.
June to August	Riding the Marches, all over Scotland.

BORDER RIDINGS AND FESTIVALS, "RIDING THE MARCHES"

The towns of the Borders have a number of annual festivals, some of which date back more than 400 years, to commemorate their history. They all take place in the summer months. The oldest of these is the Lauder Common Riding. The Braw Lads' Gathering in Galashiels (established in 1939), the Hawick Common Riding (established 1703), the Lauder Common Riding (established 1686), Jedburgh Callants Festival (established 1947), Coldstream Civic Week (established 1952), Duns Summer Festival (established 1949) and Kelso Civic Week (established 1937) all involve rideouts, which also take place at Peebles in Beltane week (above). The celebrations are marked with historic ceremonies, parades, competitions and dances.

June	Lanimer Day, Lanark, Lanarkshire, on the Thursday between the sixth and twelfth days of June. Festivities have extended to take in the whole week.
June, mid month	Guid Nychburris, Dumfries, encouraging neighbourliness.
June, Third Week	Beltane Festival, Peebles, Borders.
June	The Braw Lads Gathering, Galashiels, Borders.
June to September	Highland games, all over Scotland.

BELTANE FESTIVAL, PEEBLES, JUNE

The fire festival of Beltane, which is thought to have originally been a pagan festival marking the coming of summer, has undergone something of a revival in various parts of Scotland in recent years. The Beltane celebrations in Peebles have been an important part of the town's calendar for hundreds of years. They used to be held at the beginning of May, but are now held in the third week in June to coincide with the Riding of the Marches. The celebrations last for one week and include races, dances, a parade and the crowning of the Beltane Queen.

THE BRAW LADS' GATHERING, GALASHIELS

A week of festivities in the Border town with events for all ages which was established in 1930. Takes place at the end of June. The highlight of the occasion is the Braw Lad, with the burgh flag, leading his riders to the Raid Stane, which marks the place where, in 1337, the men from Gala defeated raiders from over the border.

July	Eyemouth Herring week.
July, last two weeks	Glasgow Fair fortnight, local trade's holiday, now includes a fairground on Glasgow Green.
August 1	Lammas, marks the beginning of autumn.
August, second week	Burryman procession, South Queensferry, Midlothian.

EYEMOUTH HERRING WEEK

Eyemouth Herring Week is held annually in July. The town is alive with dances, competitions and parades during the week and the highlight is the crowning of the elected Herring Queen.

THE FERRY FAIR, SOUTH QUEENSFERRY –
THE BURRY MAN

The Ferry Fair is held in the second week of August and every year the council of South Queensferry awards a local man the honour of being the Burry Man. It's not an easy job – it requires a good deal of stamina and a good level of heat tolerance. and, inevitably, (it is a Scottish tradition) a strong head for alcohol. The Burry Man has to make his own costume – from head to foot, he is dressed in a flannel suit to which has been attached thousands of burrs – the fruit of the Lesser Burdock plant – which he is supposed to pick himself. With everything covered in burrs and decorative flowers (leaving holes for his nose, mouth and eyes) he looks a strange sight indeed. His task is to parade around the town on the appointed day, calling at all local hostelries and a number of other local businesses for refreshment on the way. The origins of the Burry Man are lost in the mists of time, although it is thought that he may be a fertility symbol, a representation of the coming harvest.

August 15	Marymas, the feast of the Virgin, Inverness and Caithness.
September, dates vary	Fisherman's Walks.
September 27	Feast of St Barr.
September 28	Michaelmas Eve.
September 29	St Michael's Day. Feast of St Michael, patron saint of the sea. Struan Michael cakes were made.
October 18	Sour Cakes Day, St Luke's Eve, Feast of St Luke, Rutherglen.
October 31	Hallowe'en, All Hallow's Eve.
November 1	All Hallows, All Saints Day.
November 5	Bonfire Night.
November 11	Martinmas. The feast of St Martin which was the traditional date for slaughter of cattle for the winter.
–	Remembrance Sunday, nearest Sunday to Armistice Day, November 11.

November 30   St Andrews Day. Our patron saint's day is now an
                     official public holiday although only as a substitute
                     for an existing local holiday..

HALLOWE'EN – SAMHAIN

Samhain was celebrated as a fire festival in Celtic times. It was
the beginning of the New Year in the Celtic calendar, when the
animals that were not to be kept for breeding were slaughtered
for meat for the winter and the people prepared for the long,
cold nights to come.

Hallowe'en was traditionally the time when demons, witches
and the spirits of the dead could roam freely amongst the living.
It was a time for caution – for appeasing vengeful spirits and for
protecting oneself from harm. Hallowe'en was also a time when
young women sought to find out who their future husband might
be, through divination, using hazelnuts, apples, etc.

The tradition of 'guising' (known nowadays as 'trick or treat')
stems from the tradition of protecting oneself from evil spirits.
Children dress up in ghoulish costumes and call upon their
neighbours, hoping for a small reward in return for a song, a
poem or a story. Nowadays, children in Scotland have adopted
the practice of making their Hallowe'en lanterns from pumpkins.
Originally, a 'neep' – a turnip – would be hollowed out for the
purpose. A popular game that is traditionally played at Hallowe'en
gatherings is 'dookin' for apples' – trying to retrieve apples from
a bowl of water using the teeth, or a fork held in between the
teeth.

December 24   Christmas Eve. Sowans nicht, a night of eating
                     sowans, i.e., oat husks and fine meal soaked
                     overnight in water.

December 25   Christmas Day. Celebrated in medieval times
                     but, during the Reformation of the sixteenth
                     century the celebration based on a pagan
                     festival was frowned upon and stopped. Its
                     renewed celebration as a Christian and public
                     holiday began as late as the mid-twentieth
                     century in Scotland.

December 26	Sweetie Scone Day.
–	The Mason's Walk, Melrose, a torchlit parade in honour of St John the Evangelist.
December 29 to 31	Hogmanay Party, Edinburgh.
December 31	Hogmanay.

HOGMANAY TRADITIONS

Cleaning

Many people still believe that the house should be thoroughly cleaned on or before Hogmanay, to get rid of the dirt of the Old Year and welcome the New Year into a clean home.

Letting the Old Year Out and the New Year In

Just before midnight, a window should be opened at each side of the house to let the Old Year out and the New Year in.

First Footing

After the New Year has been 'brought in', it is customary to pay the first visit of the year to friends and neighbours and in turn, to welcome people into your home for a New Year's drink and a bite to eat. Ideally, the first caller to your home after the New Year should be tall and dark-haired. First-footers should always bring something with them when they call upon their neighbours. Traditionally, the first-footer's gifts should be a piece of coal – to bring warmth to the home, a bottle of whisky and something to eat – to bring plenty to eat and drink in the coming year.

Auld Lang Syne

Auld Lang Syne is traditionally sung after the bells have rung and everybody has been wished a Happy New Year.

AULD LANG SYNE

'Auld Lang Syne' has become a must for New Year's celebrations the world over, particularly in Scotland, the country where it was first written and sung. Although Robert Burns did not claim that the song was entirely his own creation – he had heard it sung before he wrote it down, many of the words of the version that is most commonly sung today are thought to have been composed by Burns himself. In spite of the fact that everybody is familiar with 'Auld Lang Syne', relatively few people know all the words to the song. In the early minutes of the New Year, all over Scotland and in other countries too, thousands of people are getting them wrong – although, admittedly, few people care. It is undoubtedly a song that is appreciated more for the sentiment it conveys than the poetry it contains.

Chorus

And for auld lang syne, my jo
For auld lang syne,
We'll tak' a cup o' kindness yet,
For auld lang syne.

1

Should auld acquaintance be forgot,
And never brought to mind?
Should auld acquaintance be forgot
And days of auld lang syne.

2

And surely ye'll be your pint-stoup
And surely I'll be mine
And we'll tak' a cup o' kindness yet,
For auld lang syne.

3

We twa hae run about the braes
And pu'd the gowans fine;
But we've wandered mony a weary foot,
Sin auld lang syne.

4

We twa hae paidl'd i' the burn,
Frae mornin' sun till dine;
But seas between us braid hae roar'd
Sin auld lang syne.

5

And there's a hand, my trusty fiere!
And gie's a hand o' thine!
And we'll tak' a right guid-willy waught,
For auld lang syne.

SAINTS WITH SCOTTISH CONNECTIONS

Saint Adamnan	Seventh century Irish monk who wrote a life of Columba. His feast day is September 23.
Saint Andrew	An apostle of Christ, crucified in Patras for his work preaching the gospel. His relics were brought to Scotland (St Andrews in Fife) by St Regulus. St Andrew is the patron saint of Scotland. His feast day is November 30.
Saint Baldred	Lived as a hermit on the Bass Rock in East Lothian in the late sixth and early seventh century. Founded a church at Tyninghame and evangelised the surrounding area. His feast day is February 6.
Saint Barr	Irish missionary who established a monastic community on the island of Barra in the early seventh century. His feast day is September 27.
Saint Blane	Miracle worker and missionary to the Picts who was born on the Isle of Bute in the sixth century. Founded the first church at Dunblane. His feast day is August 11.
Saint Boisil	An abbot of Melrose who lived in the seventh century. The town of St Boswell's is named after him. His feast day is February 23rd.
Saint Brendan	An Irish saint of the sixth century, who visited and preached in the Western Isles. He embarked upon a legendary voyage, which may have taken him as far as America. He is known as Brendan the Navigator, or Brendan the Voyager. His feast day is April 16.
Saint Bride	(Bridget) Irish saint of the fifth century who was also revered in Scotland. Her feast day is February 1.
Saint Columba	(Columcille) Lived 521–597. An Irish missionary

who founded the monastery of Derry before coming to Scotland. From his base on the island of Iona, he worked to spread Christianity through the north and west of Scotland. His feast day is June 9.

Saint Comgall
Irish monk who founded the abbey of Bangor. He came to Scotland where he worked with St Columba and lived on the island of Tiree. He died in 603. His feast day is October 7.

Saint Comgan
An Irish prince of the eighth century who came to Scotland to follow the monastic life. His feast day is May 12.

Saint Cuthbert
Missionary, healer and teacher who was educated at Melrose. Became bishop of Hexham then of Lindisfarne. He died in 687. The town of Kirkcudbright is named after him. His feast day is March 20.

Saint Devenick
A missionary of the ninth century who founded churches at Lower Banchory and Methlick. His feast day is November 13.

Saint Donan
Irish missionary who lived in a monastic community on the island of Eigg and was murdered by Vikings in 618. His feast day is April 16.

Saint Drostan
Founder of the original monastery of Deer in the sixth century. He is the patron saint of Aberlour. His feast day is December 14.

Saint Duthac
A bishop of Ross who died in 1065. He is the patron saint of Easter Ross. His feast day is March 8.

Saint Ebba the Elder
(Lived c. 615-683) A Northumbrian Princess who converted to Christianity after coming to Scotland. She became a nun and founded the abbey of Coldingham. Her feast day is August 25.

Saint Ebba the Younger
An abbess of Coldingham who died when Vikings burned the convent in 870. Her feast day is August 23.

Saint Enoch
(or St Thenew) The daughter of a king of Lothian in the sixth century. She gave birth to St Kentigern (or St Mungo) on the island of Culross. Her feast day is July 18th.

Sain Erchard
Also known as M'erchaid. Lived and preached in

Deeside and founded a church at Kircardine o'Neill. His feast day is August 24.

Saint Fechan or Vigean Irish saint of the mid-seventh century. Associated with Ecclefechan and Arbroath.

Saint Fergus A missionary who preached in the north of Scotland, particularly in Caithness. The town of St Fergus near Peterhead is named after him.

Saint Fillan of Loch Earn A saint of the fifth century. St Fillans on Loch Earn is named after him.

Saint Fillan of Strathfillan The son of an Irish prince of the 8th century who established a monastery at Strathfillan. He cured the sick, using healing stones. His feast day is January 9.

Saint Gilbert A thirteenth-century bishop of Caithness and a staunch defender of Scotland's independence. He died in 1245. His feast day is April 1.

Saint Giles A Greek missionary who lived around the seventh century. He travelled to France to preach and spent much of his time administering to the poor. He is the patron saint of beggars and the patron saint of Edinburgh and Elgin. His feast day is September 1.

Saint Inan A ninth century monk who lived as a hermit near Irvine in Ayrshire. His feast day is August 18.

Saint John An apostle of Christ. He is the patron saint of Perth. His feast day is December 27.

Saint John Ogilvie A priest from Keith who was tortured and killed in 1615 for ministering to persecuted Catholics in Scotland. His feast day is March 8.

Saint Kentigern Also known as St Mungo. A missionary, taught by St Serf, who founded the city of Glasgow. He is the patron saint of Glasgow. His feast day is July 1.

Saint Kessog Missionary saint of the sixth century. He is the patron saint of Lennox. His feast day is March 8.

Saint Leonard A monk who lived in Germany in the sixth century. He was venerated at St Andrews. His feast day is November 6.

Saint Machar (originally calle Mochreiha) A missionary of the sixth century who was sent by Columba to preach on Deeside. He is the patron saint of Aberdeen. His feast day is November 12.

Saint Magnus Erlandsson	A ruler of Orkney who was murdered in 1118 by his cousin. St Magnus Cathedral was built in his honour.
Saint Maol Rubha	An Irish missionary of the seventh century who founded a church at Applecross. His feast day is August 27.
Saint Margaret of Scotland	(Lived 1046–1093) The wife of Malcolm ('Canmore') III. She was a profoundly religious woman, who brought Benedictine monks to Scotland. Her feast day is November 16.
Saint Mary	The virgin mother of Jesus Christ. She is the patron saint of Dundee. Her feast day is July 22.
Saint Mirren	(Mirin) An Irish abbot who came to Scotland and founded the first church of Paisley. The island of Inchmurrin in Loch Lomond is named after him. He is the patron saint of Paisley. His feast day is September 15.
Saint Molaise	Irish saint who came to Scotland and lived in a cave on the Holy Island, off the coast of Arran. His feast day is September 12.
Saint Moluag	A contemporary of Columba who brought Christianity to the Island of Lismore and parts of the north east of Scotland. His feast day is June 25.
Saint Monan	A seventeenth-century missionary monk who preached in Fife. He was murdered by Vikings. The town of St Monans is named after him. His feast day is March 1.
Saint Nathalan	A seventhth-century bishop of Aberdeen who established a number of churches in the area, eg at Old Meldrum and Tullich. He died in 678. His feast day is January 8.
Saint Nicholas	Greek saint of the fourth century, nowadays identified with Santa Claus. He is the patron saint of Aberdeen. His feast day is December 6.
Saint Ninian	Lived in the beginning of the fifth century. Born in Rome, and travelled to Scotland to bring the message of the gospel. Established the first Christian church in Scotland in Whithorn, Galloway. His feast day is August 26.
Saint Patrick	A fifth-century missionary to Ireland whose

	relationship with Scotland is uncertain. He may have been born in Kilpatrick, near Dumbarton. His feast day is March 7.
Saint Regulus	Also known as St Rule. Greek monks who brought the relics of St Andrew to Scotland in the middle of the 4th century.
Saint Serf	Leader of the monastic community at Culross in the sixth century, who taught St Kentigern and gave him the name Mungo. He is the patron saint of Shetland. His feast day is July 1.
Saint Ternan	A contemporary of St Serf who lived in the monastery at Culross and may have taught St Kentigern. He died in 583. His feast day is June 12.

DEADLY LEGACY
Did you know ... ?

The entire crew of the Enola Gay, the plane which dropped the American atomic bomb on Hiroshima, Japan during the Second World War, were of Scots descent.

NOBEL PRIZE WINNERS BORN IN SCOTLAND

It is claimed that there have been as many as fifty Nobel Prize winners of Scots descent. Certainly, the lists of winners in all categories contain many Scottish names – McMillan, Langmuir, McClintock, etc. The following is a list of those whose claim to Scottishness lies not in the blood of their near or distant forebears, but in the place of their birth.

Chemistry

Sir William Ramsay, 1904

Alexander Robertus Todd, Baron Todd of Trumpington, 1957

Economics

Sir James Alexander Mirrlees 1996

Peace

Arthur Henderson, 1934
Lord John Boyd Orr ,1949

Physics

Charles Thomson Rees Wilson, 1927

Physiology/Medicine

John J R MacLeod, 1928
Sir Alexander Fleming, 1945
Sir James Black, 1988

LOCH LOMOND

'Loch Lomond' is a song that is familiar to thousands of people all around Scotland. The legend behind the song is less well known. It is said that the song was written around the time of the '45 Jacobite rebellion, when many Scots soldiers were imprisoned in Carlisle, over the border from their beloved country. Eventually, some of them were released, but others were less fortunate and were executed. The song is written from the point of view of one of the less fortunate soldiers. He is addressing a friend who is about to be released. The words of the song, 'ye'll tak the high road and I'll tak' the low road', reflect a popular belief at the time about the spirits of the dead. If a person died far away from home, their spirit was believed to travel by a spiritual path, known as 'the Low Road', back to the place of their birth to rest. The soldier who is about to die remembers his sweetheart whom he left at Loch Lomondside and whom he will never see again. He tells his friend that he will return to Scotland, but that his road – the low road – is faster and will get him there first.

1

By yon bonnie banks and by yon bonnie braes,
Where the sun shines bright on Loch Lomond,
Where me and my true love were ever wont to gae
On the bonnie, bonnie banks of Loch Lomond.

Chorus

Oh, ye'll tak' the high road
And I'll tak' the low road,
And I'll be in Scotland afore ye,
But me and my true love will never meet again
On the bonnie, bonnie banks of Loch Lomond.

2

'Twas there that we parted in yon shady glen
On the steep, steep, sides of Ben Lomond,
Where in the purple hue, the Highland hills we view
And the moon comin' out in the gloamin'.
   Chorus

3

The wee birdies sing and the wild flowers spring
And in sunshine the waters are sleepin';
But the broken heart it kens nae second Spring again,
Tho' the waefu' may cease frae their greetin'.
   Chorus

A HIGHLAND GRACE

O Lord, when hunger pinches sore,
Do Thou stand us in good stead
And send us from Thy bounteous store
A tup or wether head.

THE FLOWER OF SCOTLAND

'Flower of Scotland' was written by the late Roy Williamson (1937–1990) who, with singing partner Ronnie Browne, achieved fame as The Corries, a Scottish folk-singing duo who were at the height of their popularity in the 1960s and '70s and whose music is still listened to and enjoyed in Scotland today.

The song, written in the 1960s, was adopted as an official anthem by Scottish Rugby Union in 1990, and by the Scottish Football Associaton for the national team in 1996, and is now generally acknowledged as Scotland's own unofficial national anthem, narrowly beating 'Scotland the Brave' (*see* page 176) into second place.

The words of the song refer to Robert the Bruce's great victory over Edward II at the Battle of Bannockburn in 1314.

1

Oh flower of Scotland
When will we see yer like again
That fought and died for
Yer wee bit hill and glen
And stood against him
Proud Edward's army
And sent him homeward
Tae think again

2

The hills are bare now
And autumn leaves lie thick and still
O'er land that is lost now
Which those so dearly held
That stood against him
Proud Edward's army
And sent him homeward
Tae think again.

3

Those days are passed now
And in the past they must remain
But we can still rise now
And be the nation again
That stood against him
Proud Edward's army
And sent him homeward
Tae think again.

SCOTLAND THE BRAVE

The career of the writer of the lyrics of 'Scotland the Brave', Clifford (or Cliff as he was better known) Hanley (1922–1999), was as versatile as it was accomplished. He was variously employed as a journalist, novelist, critic, broadcaster, playwright, songwriter and was also a confident and much-loved performer and public speaker. His songwriting career began when, in December 1951, he was asked by the late Robert Wilson, then a well-known Scottish singer, who at the time was performing in a musical show at the Glasgow Empire, to write words to accompany an old highland pipe tune. The song, 'Scotland the Brave', was used to close the first half of the show and it went on to be a hit all over the world. Hanley's songwriting continued in partnership with the late Ian Gourlay, a Scottish musician and composer, and they wrote a number of comedy songs.

Cliff Hanley's first book was *Dancing in the Streets*, a memoir of growing up in Glasgow's east end, which was followed by *Another Street, Another Dance*. His novels include *The Taste of Too Much*, *The Red-haired Bitch* and *Love From Everybody*. From 1979 to 1980 he was writer in residence at York University Toronto and from 1965 to 1972 he was member of the Scottish Arts council. He died in 1999.

1

Hark when the night is falling
Hear! hear the pipes are calling,
Loudly and proudly calling,
Down thro' the glen.
There where the hills are sleeping,
Now feel the blood a-leaping,
High as the spirits of the old Highland men.

Chorus:
Towering in gallant fame,
Scotland my mountain hame!
High may your proud standards
    gloriously wave!
Land of my high endeavour,
Land of the shining river,
Land of my heart for ever!
Scotland the brave!

2

High in the misty Highlands,
Out by the purple islands,
Brave are the hearts that beat
Beneath Scottish skies.
Wild are the winds to meet you,
Staunch are the friends that greet you,
Kind as the love that shines from fair maiden's eyes.

3

Far off in sunlit places,
Sad are the Scottish faces,
Yearning to feel the kiss
Of sweet Scottish rain.
Where tropic skies are beaming,
Love sets the heart a-dreaming,
Longing and dreaming for the homeland again.

4

Hot as a burning ember,
Flaming in bleak December
Burning within the hearts
Of clansmen afar!
Calling to home and fire,
Calling the sweet desire,
Shining a light that beckons from every star!

Music traditional, lyrics by Cliff Hanley 1951.

TOASTS

Slàinte!

(Gaelic: health)

Here's tae us,
Wha's like us –
Damn few,
An' they're a' deid –
Mair's the pity.

Unknown

Up wi' your glasses, an' Deil tak the
hindmaist!

{*Poss. from Burns, Address to the Haggis*}

May the best you've ever seen
Be the worst you'll ever see,
May a moose ne'er leave your girnal
Wi' a teardrop in his e'e;
May ye aye keep hale and hearty
Till ye're auld enoug tae dee,
May ye aye be just as happy
As I wish ye aye tae be.

Allan Ramsay

Blythe may we a' be
Ill may we never see.

Trad.

Here's tae grand luck,
And muckle fat weans!

Trad.

I drink to the health of another
And the other I drink to is he –
In the hope that he drinks to another
And the other he drinks to is me.

Unknown

May the hinges of friendship never rust
Or the wings of love lose a feather.

Dean Ramsey

UK NUMBER ONE SINGLES FEATURING SCOTTISH ARTISTS, 1957–2004

April 1960	Lonnie Donegan	'My Old Man's A Dustman' (4 weeks)
January 1969	Marmalade	'Ob-La-Di-Ob-La-Da' (2 weeks)
June 1971	Middle of the Road	'Chirpy Chirpy Cheep Cheep' (5 weeks)

Oct/Nov 1971	Rod Stewart	'Maggie May' (4 weeks)
April/May 1972	The Pipes and Drums of the Military Band of the Royal Scots Dragoon Guards	'Amazing Grace' (5 weeks)
September 1972	Rod Stewart	'You Wear It Well' (1 week)
January 1973	The Sweet	'Blockbuster' (1 week)
February 1975	Pilot	'January' (3 weeks)
March 1975	Bay City Rollers	'Bye Bye Baby' (6 weeks)
July 1975	Bay City Rollers	'Give a Little Love' (3 weeks)
September 1975	Rod Stewart	'Sailing' (4 weeks)
November 1975	Billy Connolly	'D.I.V.O.R.C.E.' (1 week)
February 1976	Slik	Forever and Ever (1 week)
January 1978	Paul McCartney and Wings (Connection: Campbeltown Pipe Band)	'Mull of Kintyre' (9 weeks)
October 1979	Lena Martell	One Day at a Time (3 weeks)
December 1978	Rod Stewart	'Do You Think I'm Sexy?' (1 week)
August 1981	Aneka	'Japanese Boy' (1 week)
July 1983	Rod Stewart	'Baby Jane' (3 weeks)
December 1984	Jim Diamond	'I Should Have Known Better' (1 week)
February 1985	Elaine Paige and Barbara Dickson	'I Knew Him So Well' (3 weeks)
July 1985	The Eurythmics (Connection: Annie Lennox)	'There Must Be An Angel' (1 week)
October 1985	Midge Ure	'If I Was' (1 week)
September 1986	The Communards (Connection: Jimmy Sommerville)	'Don't Leave Me This Way' (4 weeks)
May 1988	Fairground Attraction (Connection: Eddie Reader)	'Perfect' (1 week)
May 1988	Wet Wet Wet	'With A Little Help From My Friends' (3 weeks)
June 1988	The Time Lords (Connection: Bill Drummond)	'Doctorin' the Tardis' (1 week)

Feb/Mar 1989	Simple Minds	'Belfast Child' (2 weeks)
February 1991	The KLF (Connection: Bill Drummond)	'3 am Eternal' (2 weeks)
January 1992	Wet Wet Wet	'Goodnight Girl' (4 weeks)
September 1992	The Shamen	'Ebeneezer Goode' (3 weeks)
April 1993	The Bluebells	'Young at Heart' (4 weeks)
October 1993	Take That with Lulu (Connection: Lulu)	'Relight My Fire' (2 weeks)
February 1994	D:Ream	'Things Can Only Get Better' (4 weeks)
June 1994	Wet Wet Wet	'Love Is All Around' (15 weeks)
December 1996	Dunblane	'Knocking on Heaven's Door' (1 week)
August 2002	Darius (Danesh)	'Colourblind' (2 weeks)
February 2003	David Sneddon	'Stop Living The Lie' (2 weeks)
January 2004	Michelle McManus	'All This Time' (3 weeks)
Jun 2006	Sandi Thom	'I Wish I Was A Punk Rocker' (1 week)
Mar 2007	The Proclaimers with Brian Potter and Andy Pipkin	'I'm Gonna Be (500 Miles)' (3 weeks)
December 2007 (Xmas No 1)	Leon Jackson	'When You Believe' (3 weeks)

OLYMPIC FACTS

- Two Scots have won three Olympic medals since 1900. Rodney Pattison won a gold medal at the Olympics in Mexico in 1968 for yachting. He repeated his success with another gold at Munich in 1972. In 1976, in Montreal, he won a silver medal. David Wilkie won a silver medal at the 1972 Olympics in Munich for the 200m Breaststroke. In 1976, in Montreal, he won a gold in the 200m Breaststroke and a silver in the 100m Breaststroke.

- 1908, 1912 and 2000 were good years for Scots Olympic athletes. In London in 1908, nine medals were won for Great Britain by Scots – four individual medals, five for team events. Five of these medals were gold. In Stockholm in 1912, nine medals came home to Scotland again, four individual, five for team events. Seven of the medals were gold. In 2000, in Sydney, the Scots had reason to celebrate for a third time, with two gold and seven silver medals.

- In the Winter Olympics of 2002, four Scotswomen had the nation glued to their television screens for a nail-biting competition for the Women's Curling gold medal. They took the match against Switzerland to a very close finish, winning 4–3 with the last stone of the game, played by the skip, Rhona Martin. The team, consisting of Rhona Martin, Fiona MacDonald, Margaret Morton, Janice Rankin and Debbie Knox, brought back the first gold medals for Britain at the Winter Olympics since Torvill and Dean's triumph in 1984.
- Great Britain's performance at the 2008 Beijing Olympics was its best in a century. Its cyclists were particularly outstanding. Of those cyclists Scotsman Chris Hoy was surely man of the games, winning three gold medals.

SCOTTISH OLYMPIC MEDAL WINNERS

Year	Venue	Name	Sport	Medal
1900	Paris	Walter Rutherford	Golf	Silver
1900	Paris	David Robertson	Golf	Bronze
1904	Athens	John McGough	1,500m	Silver
1904	Athens	Wyndham Halswelle	400m	Silver
1904	Athens	Wyndham Halswelle	800m	Bronze
1908	London	Arthur Robertson	Team Steeplechase	Gold
1908	London	Wyndham Halswelle	400m	Gold
1908	London	Angus Gillan	Coxless Fours	Gold
1908	London	George Cornet	Water Polo	Gold
1908	London	Royal Clyde YC	12 Meters Class	Gold
1908	London	Arthur Robertson	Steeplechase	Silver
1908	London	Alex McCulloch	Single Sculls	Silver
1908	London	Hugh Roddin	Featherweight Boxing	Bronze
1908	London	Scottish Team	Hockey	Bronze
1912	Stockholm	Henry MacKintosh	100m	Gold
1912	Stockholm	Philip Fleming	Rowing Eights	Gold
1912	Stockholm	Angus Gillan	Rowing Eights	Gold
1912	Stockholm	William Kinnear	Single Sculls	Gold
1912	Stockholm	Robert Murray	Small Bore Shooting	Gold
1912	Stockholm	George Cornet	Water Polo	Gold
1912	Stockholm	Isabella Moore	100m Freestyle Swimming	Gold
1912	Stockholm	John Sewell	Tug of War	Silver

1912	Stockholm	James Soutter	400m Relay	Bronze
1920	Antwerp	Robert Lindsay	400m Relay	Gold
1920	Antwerp	John Sewell	Tug of War	Gold
1920	Antwerp	William Peacock	Water Polo	Gold
1920	Antwerp	James Wilson	Cross Country Team	Silver
1920	Antwerp	Alexander Ireland	Welterweight Boxing	Silver
1920	Antwerp	James Wilson	10,000m	Bronze
1920	Antwerp	George McKenzie	Bantamweight Boxing	Bronze
1924	Paris	Eric Liddell	400m	Gold
1924	Paris	James McNabb	Coxless Fours	Gold
1924	Paris	James McKenzie	Lightweight Boxing	Silver
1924	Paris	Eric Liddell	200m	Bronze
1924	Paris	Archie MacDonald	Freestyle Wrestling	Bronze
1928	Amsterdam	Ellen King	100m Backstroke	Silver
1928	Amsterdam	Ellen King	100m Freestyle Relay	Silver
1928	Amsterdam	Sarah Stewart	100m Freestyle Relay	Silver
1948	London	Alistair McCorquodale	4 x 100m Relay	Silver
1948	London	David Brodie	Hockey Team	Silver
1948	London	Robin Lindsay	Hockey Team	Silver
1948	London	William Lindsay	Hockey Team	Silver
1948	London	George Sime	Hockey Team	Silver
1948	London	Neil White	Hockey Team	Silver
1948	London	Catherine Gibson	400m Freestyle Swimming	Bronze
1952	Helsinki	Douglas Stewart	Equestrian Showjumping	Gold
1952	Helsinki	Stephen Theobald	Hockey Team	Bronze
1952	Helsinki	Helen Gordon	200m Breaststroke	Bronze
1956	Melbourne	Dick McTaggart	Lightweight Boxing	Gold
1956	Melbourne	John McCormack	Lightmiddleweight Boxing	Bronze
1960	Rome	Dick McTaggart	Lightweight Boxing	Bronze
1964	Tokyo	Bobby McGregor	100m Freestyle Swimming	Silver
1968	Mexico	Rodney Pattison	Yachting, Flying Dutchman	Gold
1972	Munich	Rodney Pattison	Yachting, Flying Dutchman	Gold

1972	Munich	David Jenkins	400m Relay Team	Silver
1972	Munich	David Wilkie	200m Breaststroke	Silver
1972	Munich	Ian Stewart	5,000m	Bronze
1976	Montreal	David Wilkie	200m Breaststroke	Gold
1976	Montreal	David Wilkie	100m Breaststroke	Silver
1976	Montreal	Rodney Pattison	Yachting, Flying Dutchman	Silver
1976	Montreal	Alan McClatchey	200m Freestyle Relay	Bronze
1976	Montreal	Gordon Downie	200m Freestyle Relay	Bronze
1980	Moscow	Alan Wells	200m	Gold
1980	Moscow	Linsey MacDonald	400m Relay Team	Bronze
1984	Los Angeles	Richard Budgett	Rowing, Coxed Four	Gold
1984	Los Angeles	Ian Stark	Equestrian 3-Day Event	Silver
1984	Los Angeles	Veryan Pappin	Hockey Team	Bronze
1984	Los Angeles	Alister Allan	Smallbore Free Rifle	Bronze
1984	Los Angeles	Neil Cochran	200m Medley Swimming	Bronze
1984	Los Angeles	Neil Cochran	200m Freestyle Relay	Bronze
1984	Los Angeles	Paul Easter	200m Freestyle Relay	Bronze
1988	Seoul	Veryan Papin	Hockey Team	Gold
1988	Seoul	Michael McIntyre	Yachting Star Class	Gold
1988	Seoul	Liz McColgan	10,000m	Silver
1988	Seoul	Elliot Bunney	4 x 100m Relay	Silver
1988	Seoul	Ian Stark	Equestrian 3-Day Event	Silver
1988	Seoul	Alister Allan	Smallbore Free Rifle	Silver
1988	Seoul	Yvonne Murray	3,000m	Bronze
1992	Barcelona	Simon Terry	Archery Individual	Bronze
1992	Barcelona	Simon Terry	Archery Team	Bronze
1992	Barcelona	Susan Fraser	Hockey Team	Bronze
1992	Barcelona	Wendy Fraser	Hockey Team	Bronze
1992	Barcelona	Alison Ramsay	Hockey Team	Bronze
1996	Atlanta	Graham Smith	1,500m Freestyle	Bronze
2000	Sydney	Andrew Lindsay	Rowing Men's Eight	Gold
2000	Sydney	Shirley Robertson	Sailing, Europe Class	Gold
2000	Sydney	Stephanie Cook	Modern Pentathlon	Gold
2000	Sydney	Chris Hoy	Cycling, Olympic Sprint Team	Silver
2000	Sydney	Craig MacLean	Cycling, Olympic Sprint Team	Silver

2000	Sydney	Ian Stark	Equestrian 3-Day Event	Silver
2000	Sydney	Gillian Lindsay	Rowing, Quadruple Sculls	Silver
2000	Sydney	Katherine Grainger	Rowing, Quadruple Sculls	Silver
2000	Sydney	Mark Covell	Sailing, Star Class	Silver
2004	Athens	Shirley Robertson	Sailing, Yngling class	Gold
2004	Athens	Chris Hoy	Cycling, Men's 1km Time Trial	Gold
2004	Athens	Katherine Grainger	Rowing, Women's Pairs	Silver
2004	Athens	Campbell Walsh	Canoeing, Men's K1 Kayak	Silver
2008	Beijing	Chris Hoy	Cycling, Men's team sprint	Gold
2008	Beijing	Chris Hoy	Cycling, Men's Sprint	Gold
2008	Beijing	Chris Hoy	Cycling, Men's Keirin	Gold
2008	Beijing	Ross Edgar	Cycling, Men's Keirin	Silver
2008	Beijing	David Florence	Canoeing, Men's Slalom C-1	Silver
2008	Beijing	Katherine Grainger	Rowing, Quadruple Sculls	Silver

HOW TO WRAP THE GREAT KILT

A great kilt, or plaid, is made from three to six yards of full-width fabric. In the 1500s to 1700 when the great kilt was worn it would not have been made of tartan fabric. Tartans and kilts were banned at this time. It would have been made from naturally-dyed wool and would therefore have been in quite dull muted colours. There is no contemporary documented technique for putting on the kilt but this is one way that is aimed at making it as straightforward as possible.

Put on the shirt and waistcoat that you intend to wear and prepare to lay out the material flat. You will also need a belt. Using the span of your hands, roughly estimate the width of your body. You will need to know this in order to divide the material into three sections lengthways.

Lay out the kilt fabric on the floor, lengthways. Using the span of your hands measure out the the width of your body.

Gather the fabric so that there are three sections. The first and third sections should be slightly wider than your body.

You are going to neatly pleat the middle section until it is roughly the same width as the other two sections.

Take a belt and slide it underneath the material. Lie down on top of the fabric with your waist at the level of the belt. The hem of the garment should just reach the centre of your knees. Wrap the right side over yourself, then wrap the left side over yourself. When you feel this is lying neatly fasten it with the belt. If you are happy that the hem is straight and level, stand up.

Take the centre of the plaid in both hands and draw backwards. Tuck the centre area of the plaid into your belt on both sides.

Hold both ends of the plaid in your left hand and draw over your left shoulder. Fasten the material to your shirt or waistcoat with a plaid brooch.

INDEX